LIFE

MERCE CUNNINGHAM

MEREDITH MONK

BILL T. JONES

art PERFORMS

Walker Art Center, Minneapolis

AT&T

May 1998

For more than fifty years, AT&T has been committed to bringing the arts to people and people to the arts. In large part, our efforts have been aimed at new forms of expression being created by contemporary artists.

In <u>Art Performs Life: Merce Cunningham/Meredith Monk/Bill T. Jones</u>, we celebrate three artists who have achieved excellence by taking their talents in unprecedented new directions. As supporters of the arts, the people of AT&T applaud them. As competitors in an industry moving in uncharted directions, we can admire even more the innovation and influence of these three artists.

AT&T is proud to support the Walker Art Center in this landmark exhibition.

C. Michael Armstrong
AT&T Chairman and Chief Executive Officer

cover: View of audience during performance of Meredith Monk's Juice (Part I), at the Solomon R. Guggenheim Museum, New York, 1969   Photographer unknown

inside front cover: Bill T. Jones   Drawing from a Survival Workshop   1993
ink on paper   Courtesy Foundation for Dance Promotion, New York

inside back cover: Meredith Monk   Study for Education of the Girlchild (Part I)   1972
watercolor on paper   Courtesy The House Foundation for the Arts, Inc.

Table of Contents

Forewords by *Kathy Halbreich* and *Philip Bither*   2
Introduction   Dancing in the Museum: The Impure Art by *Sally Banes*   10

Merce   Cunningham
    Curator's introduction by *Philippe Vergne*   16
    Selected texts by *Merce Cunningham*   18
    Interview by *Laura Kuhn*   22
    Plates   44

Meredith   Monk
    Curator's introduction by *Siri Engberg*   66
    Interview by *Deborah Jowitt*   68
    Interview by *Jamake Highwater*   80
    Plates   94

Bill   T.   Jones
    Curator's introduction by *Kellie Jones*   116
    Interview by *Ann Daly*   118
    Interview by *Thelma Golden*   126
    Plates   136

Artists' Chronologies   158
Selected Reading List   174

Foreword

The Walker Art Center has played a singular role among cultural institutions in providing opportunities for our audiences to chart the creative endeavors and overlapping concerns of visual, performing, and media artists while commissioning new work across disciplines. As the only museum in this country persistently engaged in establishing the relationship among the artistic activities that occur in the light and dark spaces of galleries and theaters, between static and moving images, between real and fictive time, I believe we also are uniquely positioned to participate in the congruence of these disciplines into the twenty-first century. Few artists have been as nimble pioneers in extending the boundaries of their art forms as Merce Cunningham, Meredith Monk, and Bill T. Jones, each of whom has been commissioned by and appeared at the Walker numerous times throughout their careers. Art Performs Life: Merce Cunningham/Meredith Monk/Bill T. Jones is being presented by the Walker as this century draws to a close, allowing us to reflect on the influence each of these innovative practitioners exerted in redefining their fields as well as to celebrate the role each has played in shaping this institution's history.

In the recent past, the Walker has mounted a number of critically acclaimed exhibitions that have investigated the blending of cross-disciplinary artistic thought. In 1993, the Walker presented In the Spirit of Fluxus, a comprehensive exhibition mapping the breadth of this lively interdisciplinary movement to which performance and action were central. In 1994, we organized a retrospective of the work of Bruce Nauman, one of this century's most aggressively multidisciplinary artists, who early in his career made performances as a means of understanding the changing nature of sculpture. As co-curators of that exhibition, Neal Benezra and I had the pleasure on opening day to find ourselves in a spirited exchange on the Walker's auditorium stage with Nauman and Meredith Monk, an early collaborator, whose own long history with the Walker was extended that same weekend with the premiere of her groundbreaking piece, Volcano Songs, co-commissioned by the Walker. For the exhibition Duchamp's Leg in 1995, Jasper Johns' set for Merce Cunningham's Walkaround Time, an examination of Duchamp's Large Glass, took center stage in the galleries in this homage to Duchamp's legacy and influence on contemporary practice. This set also appears in the current exhibition, representing one of many moments in which the visual and performing arts have intersected in Cunningham's experimental oeuvre. Most recently, the Walker mounted a retrospective of the multiples of Joseph Beuys, a body of work replete with the notion of art and action as a metaphor for living. Bill T. Jones, whose work has been seen at the Walker five times to date, has explored most eloquently the ways in which art history, autobiography, and the pressing issues of a specific moment in history can be integrated to create stirring stage works. While in Minneapolis for performances of Still/Here in 1994, a work for which Jones used videotapes of participants from workshops for the terminally ill, he conducted a survival workshop at Pathways.

While all of these exhibitions have suggested the intertwining of the visual and performing arts, it is only now that we have fully crossed the traditional separation between the museum's space and the stage in organizing a presentation that brings the performing arts directly into the galleries. We knew this was a risky curatorial undertaking, one that would require developing a new conceptual model for mounting exhibitions. As the home of the largest museum-based performing arts department in the country, we thought it not only fitting but necessary to select artists who, because of their particularly strong ties to this institution, would be willing to share these creative risks with us. Cunningham, Monk, and Jones were the obvious choices as their collective achievements span more than thirty years of exploration at the Walker. I am extremely indebted to them for their deep involvement in this project and the accompanying residencies. They were fearless, exacting, and liberating collaborators in this experiment. I am particularly appreciative of the time they took away from their own creative endeavors to work closely with us on this exhibition.

For helping us to realize our aspirations, I am enormously grateful for the intellectual and financial generosity of AT&T, which bolstered the project at an early stage in our planning with critical funding. The devotion of Suzanne M. Sato, AT&T Vice President, Arts and Culture, made the breadth of our ambition possible. Additional support from the National Endowment for the Arts, Dayton's Frango® Fund, Goldman, Sachs & Co., and Voyageur Companies allowed us to pursue a project of this scope. I extend special thanks as well to Sage and John Cowles, longtime friends of the Walker, whose generosity and commitment to the performing arts have made the related performances and residencies by each of the artists a reality. This exhibition is also made possible by generous support from the Lila Wallace-Reader's Digest Fund, and this publication is made possible in part by a grant from the Andrew W. Mellon Foundation.

For conceiving an exhibition that would not only highlight the cross-disciplinary work of these three artists, but also engage the collaborative efforts of our staff across curatorial departments, I am grateful for the inspired leadership of our curatorial team: Visual Arts Curator Philippe Vergne, Assistant Curator Siri Engberg, and Guest Curator Kellie Jones, who researched, selected, and assembled the sections on the work of Cunningham, Monk, and Jones, respectively. Their efforts and the accompanying publication were supported by the tenacity and care of Visual Arts Curatorial Intern Jenelle Porter. Performing Arts Curator Philip Bither, Program Administrator Julie Voigt, and Assistant Program Manager Douglas Benidt, who coordinated the artists' residencies and performances during the run of the exhibition, also were informed and devoted contributors to the project. Similarly, Steve Dietz, Director of New Media Initiatives, and his staff worked hard to make visible the process by which the artists' work comes to life on our Web site (www.walkerart.org) so visitors can share aspects of this exhibition globally.

We hope this exhibition, four years in the making, will serve as a model for other multidisciplinary endeavors, linking the concerns of both artists and audiences across the creative fields. I can't imagine another institution with the history and talent necessary to undertake such a project, and I am thankful to former director Martin Friedman and the Walker's Board of Trustees, who saw early on the importance of supporting a museum that sheltered artists as well as objects, and built a collection that houses examples of the visual, performing, and media arts of our time.

Kathy Halbreich
Director, Walker Art Center

Foreword

"Three well-mannered anarchists will try to blow up a wall in Minneapolis tonight. The anarchists are choreographer Merce Cunningham, composer John Cage, and painter Robert Rauschenberg. The wall . . . is the high one between 'art' and 'life.'"
— *Minneapolis Tribune*, 1963

It is hard to imagine what dance and performance work would be like in America today were it not for the extraordinary innovations forged by Merce Cunningham, Meredith Monk, and Bill T. Jones. While their approaches and aesthetics are dissimilar, they share an essential trait: each has helped bring "art" and "life" into closer proximity, insisting that the process and final product of contemporary arts creation establish a more vital relationship with everyday life. This development has had a remarkably invigorating influence on contemporary dance, experimental theater, performance, and new-music forms.

Cunningham stripped modern dance of all artifice and narrative, psychological meaning and metaphor, thereby creating a choreographed world more directly linked with the reality of contemporary existence. His incorporation of chance and random elements and the chaos increasingly felt throughout the postwar world further connected art with life. Monk's abandonment of traditional theater spaces, her inclusion of nonprofessional actors and dancers, and the ritualistic, almost folk-like quality of her work, which is filtered through the power of collective memory, further strengthened the bond between art and life. "She opens our eyes," wrote dance critic Deborah Jowitt, "to the prevalence of miracles and the miraculousness of everyday life." Jones, who confronted issues of race, politics, sex, rage, and power in his work, without sacrificing artistic "purity" or formal concerns, also brought central issues of life back into art. He examined subjects that "united us outside of the aesthetic." His use of both text and movement for the delivery of ideas and his incorporation of his own personal truth (presaging much of identity politics of the 1980s and 1990s) further linked the worlds of life and art.

The exhibition Art Performs Life: Merce Cunningham/Meredith Monk/Bill T. Jones not only traces the development of these artists and their forms but also offers historical insight on the performing arts programming at the Walker Art Center, which began with a small series of chamber music concerts in the 1940s and blossomed into a full-fledged multidisciplinary department in 1970 under the direction of Curator Sue Weil. It was during this era that the Walker's commitment to modern dance was cemented with the beginning of longstanding commissioning/presenting relationships with Cunningham, Trisha Brown, Judson Dance Theater, Twyla Tharp, and many others. In the 1970s and 1980s, the department grew into not just the largest, but the most prestigious museum-based performing arts program in the country, actively engaged in the commissioning, presenting, and development of contemporary work across and between the disciplines.

The relationships that this institution has had with Cunningham, Monk, and Jones are deep and rich ones, spanning decades. Merce Cunningham and his company first came to the Twin Cities under the auspices of the Walker in 1963 (along with collaborators John Cage and Robert Rauschenberg). The company would return a dozen times in the coming thirty years, sometimes for residencies that lasted more than a month, at other times to premiere new works commissioned by the Walker, such as <u>Fabrications</u> (1987), <u>Field and Figures</u> (1989), and <u>Doubletoss</u> (1993). The company presented <u>Event for the Garden</u>, with a newly commissioned electronic score by Chicago composer Jim O'Rourke, in the Minneapolis Sculpture Garden in September 1998. Over the past twenty-four years, the Walker has commissioned five major pieces by Meredith Monk and has presented her work seven times, including the mounting of her epic operas <u>Education of the Girlchild</u> (1973), <u>Quarry</u> (1976), and <u>ATLAS</u> (1991). Most recently, the Walker commissioned her acclaimed music-theater work <u>The Politics of Quiet</u> (1996) as well as a new piece entitled <u>Magic Frequencies</u> to premiere in 1999. During her 1998 residency, she performed <u>A Celebration Service</u> (1996) with her vocal ensemble. Bill T. Jones and Arnie Zane were first presented by the Walker in 1981 as part of the New Dance USA Festival featuring important emerging artists. Jones and the company have returned five times, including the mounting of his massive community-based projects <u>The Promised Land</u>, which developed into <u>Last Supper at Uncle Tom's Cabin/The Promised Land</u> (1990), and <u>Still/Here</u> (1994), works co-commissioned by the Walker in partnership with Northrop Auditorium that have gone on to be acclaimed as modern masterworks. His residency in the fall of 1998 in conjunction with the exhibition, which included the presentation of <u>We Set Out Early . . . Visibility Was Poor</u> (1997), marked the start of a four-year commitment by the Walker to the company, involving annual extended residencies as well as commissions, presentations, and the development of works-in-progress.

Contemporary art centers expect and encourage experimentation, challenge, even controversy. This philosophical commitment, combined with the capacity to provide artists with substantial and sustained support (sometimes across decades), has created a uniquely nurturing atmosphere at the Walker, one that can allow some of our most daring artists to realize their largest-scale visions while protecting them from the winds of popularity and the dictates of box office. The exhibition <u>Art Performs Life</u> allows us a closer proximity with three of these seminal artists and an understanding of this institution's legacy of belief in new work.

Philip Bither
Curator, Performing Arts Department

Acknowledgments

Organizing an exhibition on three landmark careers in the performing arts—each remarkably different from the others—for presentation in museum galleries was a challenging and exciting curatorial endeavor, and one that could not have been achieved without the support and collaboration of a great many individuals. It is our hope that <u>Art Performs Life: Merce Cunningham/Meredith Monk/Bill T. Jones</u> helps to set the stage for an increased presence of cross-disciplinary exhibitions in the museum arena as we enter a new century.

At the Cunningham Dance Foundation, we extend our gratitude to William Cook, Executive Director, and David Vaughan, Archivist, who provided assistance and expertise throughout the life of the project. David Covey, Production Manager, Anna Brown, Film and Video Distribution Coordinator, Suzanne Gallo, Costume Supervisor/Costume Designer Coordinator, and Sonya Robbins, Project Coordinator, also offered important guidance, and we are grateful for their assistance. Many lenders allowed key works to be included in this presentation, and we extend our appreciation to them. In addition, Cunningham's section of the exhibition would not have been possible without the generous contribution of time and resources from Rei Kawakubo, Johanne S. Siff, and Miki Higasa at Comme des Garçons, New York; Jean Rigg of the David Tudor Estate; Johanna VanDerBeek; Charles Atlas; Elliot Caplan; Leonardo Drew; and Mark Francis at the Andy Warhol Museum.

At Meredith Monk/The House Foundation for the Arts, Inc. we salute Barbara Dufty, Managing Director, for her attention to countless questions and requests, as well as her generous support and input during all stages of exhibition planning. Michou Szabo and Brenda Cummings offered unflagging assistance in securing photographs and extensive archival material and loans. For her crucial contributions to the early organization of Monk's section of the exhibition, we are indebted to Kerry McCarthy. Amy Santos, Company Manager, and her successor, Beverly Lewis, provided valuable assistance in the organization of Monk's 1998 artist-in-residence activities at the Walker in conjunction with the exhibition. Paul Krajniak, Executive Director, the James Lovell Museum of Science, Economics, and Technology in Milwaukee, was instrumental to the process of shaping the installation. His sensitive design contributions and creative support were essential to the project's success.

At the Bill T. Jones/Arnie Zane Dance Company, Bjorn G. Amelan, Associate Director, advised us on myriad aspects of the exhibition and was a key player in the development of Jones' 1998 artist residency at the Walker. Special thanks must also go to Jodi Pam Krizer, Executive Director, who helped all along the way with the exhibition and the residency. Gregory Bain, Production Director, was indispensable, graciously assisting us with numerous trips to the storage vaults, as well as with the scouring of files and precious archives for the sake of this project. He was also the lifeline to the many composers and designers who have collaborated over the years with the company. Leah Haynes, Office Manager, assisted with research, requests, and most importantly, kept us in touch with all at the company, and we graciously acknowledge her attention to all fronts. Kimberly Palma, Lighting Supervisor, Kelly Atallah, Production Stage Manager, and James Irvine assisted with the initial research through the archival storage. Thanks also to Jonathan Green at the University of California, Riverside, who was extremely helpful with loans from the Arnie Zane Archives.

We are particularly grateful to those who have contributed texts to this book: Laura Kuhn; Deborah Jowitt; Jamake Highwater; Thelma Golden; and Ann Daly for their interviews; and Sally Banes, whose insightful essay introduces this volume. Each contributor has helped to enrich and enliven the public discourse around these innovators.

Special thanks are due to a number of colleagues at the Walker Art Center whose support made this exhibition and publication possible. We are grateful for the vision of former Walker curators John Killacky and Elizabeth Armstrong, whose essential contributions at the project's outset provided us with important groundwork from which we could further shape and refine the exhibition. Bobbi Tsumagari, Interim Curator of Performing Arts, was also of great assistance at this stage. Philip Bither, Walker Curator of Performing Arts, was an invaluable partner and collaborator. We are grateful for his contribution to the catalogue and for the work that he and his staff did to make this project truly interdisciplinary. Thanks in this regard are also due to Bruce Jenkins, Walker Curator of Film/Video, for his commitment to these artists, which has led to a film and video series during the exhibition; and to Karen Moss, Director of Education and Community Programs, and her staff for coordinating a broad range of exhibition-related programs. Director Kathy Halbreich and Chief Curator Richard Flood supported this project with reliable guidance and insight.

National Endowment for the Arts Curatorial/Education Intern Anastasia Shartin provided invaluable organization during the early stages of this project, and her work was continued through the extraordinary efforts of her successor, Jenelle Porter, who rose to the occasion to become our full collaborator on every aspect of the exhibition and publication. Visual Arts Assistants Lisa Middag and Henrietta Dwyer ably attended to innumerable administrative details surrounding the exhibition. Special thanks go to Designer Conny Purtill, who has designed this volume with sensitivity and engagement and has made valuable contributions in the many stages of the exhibition's design. Publications Manager Michelle Piranio and Editors Kathleen McLean and Pamela Johnson invested countless hours and much insight to shape the publication. In the Director's Office, Howard Oransky provided important guidance with program planning and budgetary assistance. The collection of the vast array of objects, performance relics, moving images, music, and documentary material that make up this exhibition could not have happened without the efforts of Registrar Gwen Bitz, who brought the material together seamlessly. For creating a memorable installation in the Walker galleries, we are indebted to Cameron Zebrun and his talented crew of exhibition technicians, and extend our special thanks to Phil Docken, Kirk McCall, Peter Murphy, and Eleanor Savage for their creative contributions and solutions to myriad complexities raised by this multidisciplinary presentation. For providing us with valuable materials charting each of the artists' rich histories with this institution, we are grateful to Archivist Jill Vetter.

Finally, we extend our most sincere thanks to Merce Cunningham, Meredith Monk, and Bill T. Jones, who have allowed us to make them the focus of this exhibition and publication. Had it not been for their support and input, a project of this scope would have been unthinkable. It was an honor for each of us to have had the pleasure of their enthusiastic collaboration and participation.

Philippe Vergne, Siri Engberg, and Kellie Jones
Exhibition Curators

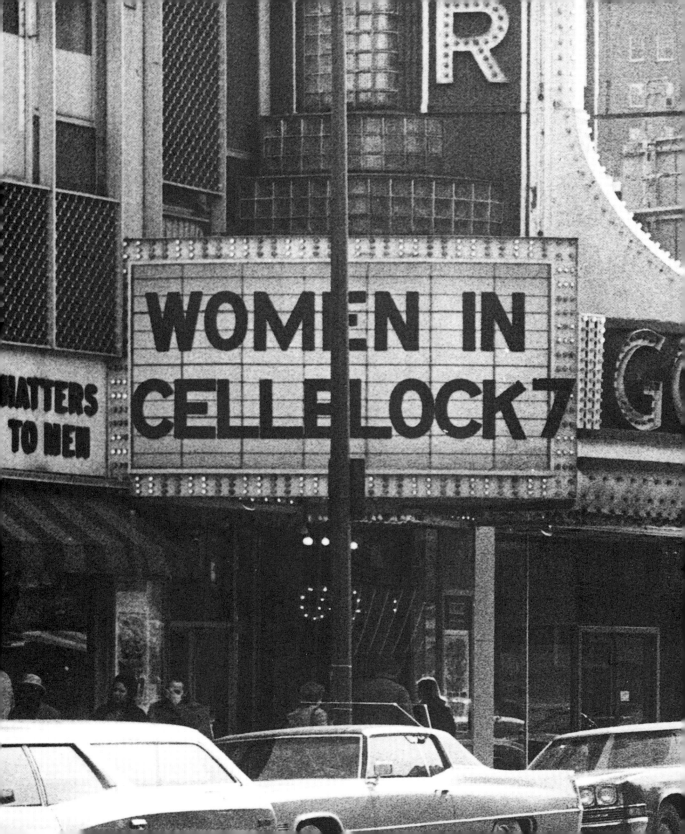

INTRODUCTION

Sally Banes is the Marian Hannah Winter Professor of Theater and Dance Studies at the University of Wisconsin, Madison, and the president of the Society of Dance History Scholars. The author of numerous books, including Terpsichore in Sneakers: Post-Modern Dance (1980), Democracy's Body: Judson Dance Theater 1962–1964 (1983) and, most recently, Dancing Women: Female Bodies on Stage (1998), her articles on dance, theater, film, and performance art have been widely published. She was formerly the performance art critic for the Village Voice and the editor of Dance Research Journal. Banes curated the Megadance program, part of the Serious Fun! Festival at Lincoln Center in New York in 1992 and 1993. She is the recipient of grants and fellowships from the National Endowment for the Humanities, the National Endowment for the Arts, and the John Simon Guggenheim Foundation, among others.

Dancing in the Museum: The Impure Art

What do Merce Cunningham, Meredith Monk, and Bill T. Jones have in common? They are three artists spanning three generations of modern and postmodern dance and performance, who have very different approaches to choreography. Since the 1940s and 1950s, Cunningham has been renowned for his brilliant technique, his use of impersonal chance and (more recently) computer composition methods, and his separation of the dancing from strict musical accompaniment. Monk, who came of age in the 1960s, is well-known for her site-specific work, her hand-crafted theatricality that verges on the mythic, and her use of both gestural movement and unusual vocal compositions. Bill T. Jones, who appeared on the national dance scene just as the 1980s began, has crafted a synthesis of virtuosity and pedestrian movement, avant-gardism and populism, formal concerns and political outcry. Certainly these three individuals seem to have followed utterly different paths, pursuing quite distinct artistic visions.

Born in Centralia, Washington, in 1919, Merce Cunningham studied tap and ballroom dancing as a child and learned Graham technique at the Cornish School. There he met the composer John Cage, with whom he collaborated for more than fifty years and whose ideas about new music and new relationships between dance and music deeply influenced his choreography. Cunningham danced in Martha Graham's company from 1939 to 1945, and he also studied at the School of American Ballet. Breaking with what had by the 1940s become the modern dance academy, he evolved his own dance technique that combined the flexible spine and strength of modern dance and the virtuosic footwork, speed, and elevation of ballet. Cage and Cunningham advocated an approach to dance-theater in which the dancing, the music, and the decor all coexisted in the same time-space continuum while maintaining their autonomy. That is, the dance wasn't choreographed to the music, nor was the music composed to the rhythms of the dancing, but both were created separately while sharing a single time frame. Influenced by Zen Buddhism and by the work and thought of Marcel Duchamp, Cage and Cunningham looked for ways to incorporate aspects of ordinary life—both sounds and movements—in their art. In the 1950s, both began using chance techniques in their work as a way to free themselves from habit as well as from personal expression, which was the dominant idiom in modern dance.

In 1954, a year after Cunningham formed his dance company, he began a ten-year collaboration with the artist Robert Rauschenberg, who not only designed costumes, decor, and lighting, but also served as technical director when the company toured. After Rauschenberg's departure in 1964, following the company's first world tour, Cunningham collaborated with many distinguished visual artists, including Jasper Johns, Frank Stella, Robert Morris, Bruce Nauman, and Andy Warhol. The ranks of composers commissioned by Cage, who served as the company's musical director until his death in 1992, include David Tudor, Morton Feldman, Christian Wolff, Gordon Mumma, Pauline Oliveros, David Behrman, Maryanne Amacher, and Takehisa Kosugi. Thus Cunningham's dance performances have always been, and continue to be, occasions for the meeting of avant-garde, abstract choreography, music, and visual art, and in fact have been instrumental in forming a community of artists in diverse fields.

Meredith Monk, born in New York City in 1942, has been a musician and dancer since childhood. Her great-grandfather was a cantor, and her mother was a professional singer. As a child, she studied eurythmics and ballet, and then majored in a combined performing arts program at Sarah Lawrence College. After graduation in 1964, she began presenting her work at Judson Church, which had recently become a lively home for experiments in dance, theater, and the visual arts. She also performed in Happenings, Off-Broadway plays, and dance works by other artists. Like Cunningham, Monk makes performances using juxtaposition and nonlinear logic, but unlike him she fuses visual, aural, and kinetic imagery for expressive effect. She is not interested in dancerly technique, preferring a more relaxed, though still stylized, way of moving. Her works are not easily categorized, although they make use of dance, theater, and song; she has called various pieces "a live movie," "a theatre cantata," "an opera epic." Often her works (like certain Asian dance-dramas, which they somewhat resemble), performed either solo or with The House, her company of singer-dancer-performers, deal with cosmic themes: spiritual crisis, vision quests, and the building of community, as in <u>Vessel</u> (1971) (about Joan of Arc), <u>Quarry</u> (1976) (about World War II), and <u>ATLAS</u> (1991) (about a woman explorer). Monk's techniques interweave the arts: in her music, the voice dances; her dancers sing; and her manipulation of space and image owe as much to film and photography as live performance.

Bill T. Jones, born in 1952 in Bunnell, Florida, grew up in a family of African-American migrant workers. The family settled in upstate New York, and Jones attended the State University of New York at Binghamton, where he studied various forms of dance: modern, Afro-Caribbean, ballet, and contact improvisation. There he was involved in various student political-protest movements in the early 1970s, and he also met Arnie Zane, a fellow student and a photographer, who became his life partner and choreographic collaborator until Zane's death in 1988. They worked at first with the American Dance Asylum (which they cofounded with

1

ohn Cage (left) and Merce Cunningham
A Dialogue at Walker Art Center, 1974

1. See RoseLee Goldberg, Performance: Live Art 1909 to the Present (New York: Abrams, 1979). Noël Carroll, in "Performance," Formations vol. 3, no.1 (Spring 1986), traces two lines of influence on contemporary American performance art: one, which he calls "art performance," derives from the concerns of visual art; the other, which he calls "performance art," derives from the avant-garde theater tradition.

2. On the collaboration of painters and poets, see Philip Auslander, The New York School Poets as Playwrights; O'Hara, Ashbery, Koch, Schuyler and the Visual Arts (New York: Peter Lang, 1989).

two other dancers in 1973), then as a duo, and then in 1982 formed the Bill T. Jones/Arnie Zane Dance Company. Jones has also performed solos throughout his career. He has collaborated with visual artists as diverse as Tseng Kwong Chi, Keith Haring, Jenny Holzer, Willi Smith, and Robert Longo, and musicians ranging from Max Roach to Julius Hemphill to Peter Gordon. Jones' dances have treated themes of racism, sexism, homophobia, and the AIDS epidemic, and his sociopolitical commitments have sometimes led him, while choreographing during residencies around the world, to draw on the participation of dancers and nondancers from local communities, as in Last Supper at Uncle Tom's Cabin/The Promised Land (1990), originally developed in Minneapolis. Still/Here (1994), a piece developed in workshops with terminally ill people and their caretakers, provoked a national debate about the purposes and meaning of both art and art criticism.

One easy answer to the question of what these apparently quite dissimilar artists have in common might be that they've all performed at the Walker Art Center. That may seem flippant, silly, or even irrelevant, yet this is a more profound matter than it appears at first glance. For the story of how dance and performance art came to be produced regularly under the auspices of art museums in the latter half of the twentieth century is an intricate one that also reveals a great deal about the individual careers of Cunningham, Monk, and Jones. And it helps explain why they all have performed at the Walker and why the vestiges of their performances would end up constituting a museum exhibition like this one.

Of course, dance, like theater, is a visual art. More so than dramatic theater, it is also a kinetic art and a musical one. Yet, for a number of diverse reasons, dance was not traditionally part of the art museum's purview. It's not just that most items in museums are static, while dance is mobile. Usually characterized as impermanent and ephemeral, dance doesn't seem to be collectible. From the curator's point of view, it is not easily shipped, stored, organized, or exhibited, because it involves bodies—persons—that are unpredictable and need to be compensated.

But in the past, even when museums occasionally presented other performing arts—say, music concerts, as the Walker itself has since 1947—or sponsored society costume balls where social dancing took place in a theatricalized party setting, or provided dancers as live entertainment at opening receptions, museums rarely presented dances as artworks for appreciation and contemplation for their own sake. And in many ways this is understandable. From the dancer's point of view, museums provide far from ideal stages. Their floors are too hard and too cold, and their galleries have no wing space or proper lighting. From the audience's point of view, the sightlines are poor, and there's standing room only. But even when art museums have had lecture halls or theaters, they are not usually properly designed or equipped for the exigencies of dancing. And finally, dance has often been considered a minor art, bordering on the decorative. The audiences for serious painting and sculpture did not necessarily overlap with audiences for dance.

However, a number of developments that took place in both dance and the visual arts over the course of the twentieth century, peaking in the United States in the 1950s and 1960s, changed all that, making the art museum a prolific producer of avant-garde dance at the height of the dance boom in the 1970s. On the dance side of the equation, an initial step was the splash made in Paris in the 1910s and 1920s by Serge Diaghilev's Ballets Russes—a modern ballet company that put leading painters and composers together with choreographers in unprecedented ways to

3. See Michael Kirby, Happenings (New York: Dutton, 1965); Thomas Kellen and Jon Hendricks, Fluxus (London and New York: Thames and Hudson, 1995); Barbara Haskell, BLAM! The Explosion of Pop, Minimalism and Performance 1958—1964 (New York: Whitney Museum and Norton, 1984); Sally Banes, Greenwich Village 1963: Avant-Garde Performance and the Effervescent Body (Durham, North Carolina: Duke University Press, 1993).

4. See Mary Emma Harris, The Arts at Black Mountain College (Cambridge, Massachusetts: MIT Press, 1987), pp. 226—228.

5. See Sally Banes, Democracy's Body: Judson Dance Theater 1962—1964 (Ann Arbor, Michigan: UMI Research Press, 1983; reprint ed. Durham, North Carolina: Duke University Press, 1993).

13

Meredith Monk and Ping Chong in Paris at Walker Art Center, 1982

create stunning total artworks. At times, the dancers even complained that the art—by the likes of Matisse, Picasso, Braque, and Miró—was upstaging the choreography. But despite the eminence of the artists, these multimedia collaborations were still situated in a theatrical, not a gallery or museum, context.

At the same time, certain avant-garde art movements began to turn to live performance (what some have called "live art" or "art performance") precisely as a way of extending ideas from painting into time and space—as the Italian Futurists did in their attempts to create representations of speed and light, or as the Bauhaus artists did in their efforts to create schematic abstractions of the human form.[1] In the 1950s and 1960s, when the center of the art world had shifted from Europe to the United States, a new generation of visual artists became intensely involved in performances of all kinds. Painters entered the theater to collaborate with poet-playwrights.[2] But also, painters and sculptors made their own non-theatrical performance artworks in galleries and art museums, inventing new, hybrid genres—Happenings, Events, Fluxus.[3]

These events had an important precedent in an untitled proto-Happening devised by composer John Cage in 1952 at Black Mountain College, the experimental college in North Carolina that since the 1930s had been an important center for artists and intellectuals. Cage's performance involved painters, musicians, poets, and a dancer doing various unconnected activities in the college dining hall, in which chairs for the spectators had been placed in a square configuration while the event took place all around and through them.[4] A number of Happenings-makers, Events artists, and Fluxus members were galvanized into action during their studies with Cage in the late 1950s.

And now the plot thickens. As visual artists moved en masse into the arena of live performance, several of them—including Robert Rauschenberg (who met Cage and Cunningham in New York in the spring of 1951), Robert Morris, Alex Hay, and Carolee Schneemann—began working in dance. No longer satisfied with working for choreographers, they decided to make dances themselves.

This was perhaps only possible because of developments in the world of early postmodern dance, where ideas about the values of traditional dance techniques and virtuosic physical training were undergoing radical questioning, at times even suggesting that dance training itself might be dispensable. At Robert Dunn's composition classes at Cunningham's studio in the early 1960s and at the Judson Dance Theater workshops that grew out of those classes, the formal emphasis was on choreographic method rather than technical prowess. And, for democratic reasons, ordinary bodies and ordinary movements were prized. Also, in a do-it-yourself spirit perfectly compatible with larger currents in the postwar American culture that celebrated volunteerism and the Horatio Alger ethic—from magazines like Popular Mechanics to government programs like the Peace Corps—artists in general challenged the status quo and hierarchical systems of licensing and approval. So suddenly, joining a group that had chosen to free itself from the constraints of specialization, visual artists without dance training credentials—but with exciting ideas about moving bodies in space—simply seized the opportunity to become dance-makers, without any authorization by the dance establishment.[5]

Once visual artists began making forays into choreography, they presented their work not only at dance concerts, but in their own world, at visual art venues—festivals, galleries, and museums. They convinced their dealers to open their showrooms to dance and performance, and art magazines like Artforum began to cover these activities on a regular basis. The painters and sculptors brought their

6. See Merce Cunningham, in conversation with Jacqueline Lesschaeve, The Dancer and the Dance (New York and London: Marion Boyars, 1985), pp. 174–177, for a description of various Events.

7. For a discussion of space and scale in Monk's work, see Brooks McNamara, "Vessel: The Scenography of Meredith Monk," The Drama Review 16 (T–53, March 1972), pp. 87–103; Sally Banes, Terpsichore in Sneakers: Post-Modern Dance (Boston: Houghton-Mifflin, 1980; 2nd ed. Middletown, Connecticut: Wesleyan University Press, 1987); and Deborah Jowitt, ed., Meredith Monk (Baltimore: Johns Hopkins University Press, 1997).

8. See Bill T. Jones, with Peggy Gillespie, Last Night on Earth (New York: Pantheon, 1995).

dance colleagues on tour and into the museums with them.

It was the entry of visual artists into dance that made art museums open their doors to dancers. But this was not just a matter of community networking. Curators and audiences saw that visual and performance artists and postmodern dancers formed a theoretical and performative continuum as the fields cross-fertilized.

The story becomes even more complicated when we consider changing attitudes toward dance spaces since mid-century. Cunningham had danced in Cage's 1952 Black Mountain event. At that same historical moment, partly as a result of the unpredictable movement choices dictated by his new use of chance techniques, Cunningham was involved in decentralizing the dance space, carrying out a frontal attack on the picture-frame perspective that had been traditional, if not de rigueur, in dance performance at least since the eighteenth century. Rather than designing well-composed pictures that guided the eye through a hierarchized space, he created an action field for dance—analogous to an Abstract Expressionist painting—that invited the spectator's eye to range freely, to wander from event to event across and around the stage.

Cunningham's students and younger colleagues at the Judson Dance Theater, a choreographic collective that presented experimental dance by artists and musicians as well as trained dancers, challenged traditional uses of space even further by rejecting conventional stages altogether. They danced purely secular dances in church sanctuaries, and also in roller-skating rinks, in lofts, and in art museums, including (in 1966) the Walker Art Center—to the consternation of critics, who found their rejection of theatrical space impertinent. Cunningham himself, by 1964, began presenting his Events— portable dances composed of newly assembled modules taken from pieces in the repertory—in unconventional spaces, including museums, gymnasiums, the Piazza San Marco in Venice, and his own dance studio classroom.[6]

Meredith Monk has been a crucial player in the transformation of the performance space. Making site-specific pieces since the 1960s, she has used the architecture of the Guggenheim Museum, the natural history displays of the Smithsonian Institution, and an abandoned hospital on Roosevelt Island (as well as unconventionally small sites), among many other "found" spaces, to create the possibility of proto-cinematic variety in scale and distance. For instance, in a section of Vessel that took place in a parking lot in New York's Soho, the seventy-five performers included pioneers sitting around campfires and a motorcycle cavalcade.[7]

Also, it was partly changes in dance technique since the 1960s—the wholesale use of relaxed, prosaic movement—that led to a veritable explosion of dancing in American and European museums in the 1970s. The risk of shinsplints was considerably diminished in pieces that mainly involved everyday locomotion—like Trisha Brown's Walking on the Wall (of the Whitney Museum)(1971)—or even total stillness—like Douglas Dunn's 101 (1974), in which he lay motionless on a large wooden structure in a Soho loft, much like a sculpture on display. But even Cunningham's dancers, employing virtuosic technique, have performed in many museums, using platforms when dancing on tile floors, to avoid injury as much as to increase visibility.

By the time Bill T. Jones and Arnie Zane began making dances in the mid-1970s in Binghamton, New York, the use of alternative spaces and nontraditional stages was the norm. The American Dance Asylum, the collective dance company they cofounded, remodeled an abandoned Elks Club for use as a dance theater. They performed at Binghamton's Experimental Television Center and visited New York City to dance at the Collective for Living Cinema, a Tribeca screening room for avant-garde film.[8] When Jones and

Thanks to Noël Carroll, Lynn Garafola, Amy Allan, and the students in my performance art seminar at the University of Wisconsin-Madison for their help on this essay.

Zane first appeared at the Walker Art Center in 1981, a regular dance season had long since been established (reaching a peak of forty-two performances in 1977) as part of a multipronged performing-arts program that included dance, theater, music, and performance-art events, not only in the museum building itself but in more conventional theater spaces. Producing dance performances had permanently entered the roster of the art museum's activities.

That Jones and Zane entered the dance world while involved in an avant-garde film, video, and photography world suggests another narrative linking Cunningham, Monk, and Jones, one about multimedia and collaboration. All three artists have worked in innovative ways with film and video—both employing these media as elements embedded in live performance and choreographing solely for the camera's eye. A pioneer in videodance, experimenting with choreography for the video camera as early as 1961, Cunningham made his first <u>Video Event</u> for television in 1974, and he has collaborated extensively with company filmmakers Charles Atlas and Elliot Caplan on dances designed specifically for the film and video cameras, some of which have been adapted to live performance. Video installations have been part of <u>Variations V</u> (1965) and, more recently, <u>Installations</u> (1996). In 1990, Cunningham began to use Life Forms®, a computer program that allows him to model movements, to assist his choreography. Monk is an accomplished film director and has incorporated film and video into her live performances since <u>16 Millimeter Earrings</u> (1966), an early solo. Jones' artistic partnership with Zane began when Zane, then a photographer, made images of Jones dancing, and Jones has choreographed for the video camera and also used video in his live work, most notably in <u>Still/Here</u>.

Bill T. Jones in <u>Break</u> at Nicollet Island Amphitheater, Minneapolis, 1981

Like Diaghilev, all three artists maximize perceptual channels on the stage to the hilt; all three inhabit interdisciplinary milieux that treat dancing as a full partner to the other arts. Monk is a polymath, a one-person collaboration (though she also works with other artists), who is as often categorized as a new-music composer or performance artist or theater director as a choreographer, and she has frequently designed the costumes and decor for her performances and directed her own films. Cunningham and Jones are dancer-choreographers who since the very beginning of their careers have worked closely with the foremost contemporary visual artists and composers of our time. (Indeed, Cunningham's company has performed at least one <u>Event</u> to Monk's music.)

Thus these three artists are important not only to the field of dance, but far beyond it, to the worlds of music, theater, film, video, computer imaging, and visual art—and to the discourse surrounding the arts. Though diverse, their visions have, in distinctive ways, always placed movement per se in larger arenas. Through their work dance has become more complex; it has exceeded the boundaries of dance movement and dance space in ways that point to limitless invention.

Like many visual artists, throughout history there have been choreographers who have perennially tried to purify their art form. But it's the hybrid nature of dance—its salutary impurity—that appeals to these three artists, though in very disparate ways. And in that sense, for them the dance event becomes not just an occasion to see dancing, but also to hear music and see art. So by bringing "dirty dancing" into the pristine cathedral of culture, they make the dance stage itself a pulsing museum of contemporary art.

Sally Banes

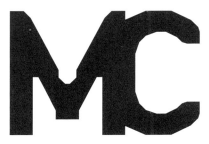

1. Merce Cunningham, <u>Changes: Notes on Choreography</u> (New York: Something Else Press, 1968).

Curator's Introduction

↴

Space, Time and Dance and Four Events That Have Led to Large Discoveries by Merce Cunningham   18

↴

Merce Cunningham in Conversation with Laura Kuhn   22
December 7, 1997   New York

"You have to love dancing to stick to it. It gives you nothing back, no manuscripts to store away, no paintings to show on walls and maybe hang in museums, no poems to be printed and sold, nothing but that single fleeting moment when you feel alive." [1]
— Merce Cunningham

It might seem paradoxical to open the chapter on Merce Cunningham with a quote that questions, perhaps, the very notion of dedicating an exhibition to him. It would seem that the first flaw of this exhibition is that it is out of sync with Cunningham himself. But we propose to show projects, rather than objects, that have challenged our way of working and thinking for nearly half a century.

The story begins between 1948 and 1952 at Black Mountain College in North Carolina with a chance meeting between John Cage, Merce Cunningham, Buckminster Fuller, Charles Olson, Robert Rauschenberg, M. C. Richards, and David Tudor. It is the story of the arts being turned upside down. In 1952 this toppling took forty-five minutes, and forty-five years later we are still trying to clarify the consequences of an untitled theater event during which Cunningham danced; John Cage, musing on the work of Antonin Artaud, gave a lecture on Master Eckhart; Robert Rauschenberg projected abstract slides and films on the walls and ceiling; M. C. Richards and Charles Olson recited texts; and David Tudor performed Cage's <u>Water Music</u>. Coffee was served, and Edith Piaf records were played. . . . The disciplines involved (dance, music, theater, poetry), without losing their specificity, were no longer the heart of the event but rather questioned the very notion of labeling. The center was lost, leaving only simultaneous agitation of meaning and the senses.

The impetus of those forty-five minutes has gained momentum over the years, often with the same accomplices, plus others: Andy Warhol, Nam June Paik, Mark Lancaster, Julian Beck and The Living Theater, Charles Atlas, Elliot Caplan, Takehisa Kosugi, Leonardo Drew, Rei Kawakubo. These numerous multidisciplinary collaborations have caused us to reconsider not only Cunningham's art, but the notion of hierarchy, any kind of hierarchy.

If Cunningham is undeniably a seminal figure in the history of dance, it is only by virtue of being contemporary, of being not only _of_ his time, but _in_ it. "More than the museum, I like the actuality," he said very early on about his involvement with technologies such as video and, more recently, computers.

So what is to be learned by seeing his work today in the context of an exhibition? The answer to this question takes the form of questions: What artist today can hope to be contemporary without addressing the issue of multi- or interdisciplinarity? What artist does not address the question of the artwork both as object and relationship? What artist does not consider the image-in-motion? What artistic institutions, inasmuch as they share the ambitions of their epoque, do not try to consider themselves that "ideal" interface between art and life, or at least host venues for productions that have not yet gained official artistic stature?

"One thing I can tell you about this dance is it has no center." This is how Cunningham described Summerspace (1958) to Rauschenberg. His statement stems from the fact that Cunningham shattered the centralized and classical spatial structure of choreography when he introduced the use of chance operations, of chaos. But, in looking at Cunningham's life work, this statement takes on another meaning, somewhere between architecture, another art of the space, and anarchy. Anarchitecture? In effect, whether it's a question of a construction or of a social construct, the central position is the weakest. The central supporting beam is the one that gives way over time. The center is the place of spineless consensus, of stagnant concession. This is what we can learn from Merce Cunningham: to be dissatisfied with existing models, with approved and easy modalities. And to try indefinitely to lose oneself, to shift one's center, or at least to alter it.

Cunningham is not merely a dancer, but so much more. What he proposes, through and beyond dance, is a radical, passionate experience whose utopian conclusion may not change the world, but suggest ways to exist in the world differently.

In his essay "The Impermanent Art" (1955), Cunningham says, "Our ecstasy in dance comes from the possible gift of freedom, the exhilarating moment that this exposing of the bare energy can give us. What is meant is not license, but freedom, that is, a complete awareness of the world and at the same time a detachment from it."

Philippe Vergne

Both texts reprinted with permission from David Vaughan, <u>Merce Cunningham: Fifty Years</u> (New York: Aperture Foundation, 1997), pp. 66–67, 276.

<u>Space, Time and Dance</u>, 1952

The dance is an art in space and time.
The object of the dancer is to obliterate that.

The classical ballet, by maintaining the image of the Renaissance perspective in stage thought, kept a linear form of space. The modern American dance, stemming from German expressionism and the personal feelings of the various American pioneers, made space into a series of lumps, or often just static hills on the stage with actually no relation to the larger space of the stage area, but simply forms that by their connection in time made a shape. Some of the space-thought coming from the German dance opened the space out, and left a momentary dealing of connection with it, but too often the space was not visual enough because the physical action was all of lightness, like sky without earth, or heaven without hell.

The fortunate thing in dancing is that space and time cannot be disconnected, and everyone can see and understand that. A body still is taking up just as much space and time as a body moving. The result is that neither the one nor the other—moving or being still—is more or less important, except it's nice to see a dancer moving. But the moving becomes more clear if the space and time around the moving are one of its opposite—stillness. Aside from the personal skill and clarity of the individual dancer, there are certain things that make clear to a spectator what the dancer is doing. In the ballet the various steps that lead to the larger movements or poses have, by usage and by their momentum, become common ground upon which the spectator can lead his eyes and his feelings into the resulting action. This also helps define the rhythm, in fact more often than not does define it. In the modern dance, the tendency or the wish has been to get rid of these "unnecessary and balletic" movements, at the same time wanting the same result in the size and vigor of the movement as the balletic action, and this has often left the dancer and the spectator slightly short.

To quibble with that on the other side: one of the best discoveries the modern dance has made use of is the gravity of the body in weight, that is, as opposite from denying (and thus affirming) gravity by ascent into the air, the weight of the body in going with gravity, down. The word "heavy" connotes something incorrect, since what is meant is not the heaviness of a bag of cement falling, although we've all been spectators of that too, but the heaviness of a living body falling with full intent of eventual rise. This is not a fetish or a use of heaviness as an accent against a predominately light quality, but a thing in itself. By its nature this kind of moving would make the space seem a series of unconnected spots, along with the lack of clear-connecting movements in the modern dance.

A prevalent feeling among many painters that lets them make a space in which anything can happen is a feeling dancers may have too. Imitating the way nature makes a space and puts lots of things in it, heavy and light, little and big, all unrelated, yet each affecting all the others.

About the formal methods of choreography—some due to the conviction that a communication of one order or another is necessary; others to the feeling that mind follows heart, that is, form follows content; some due to the feeling that the musical form is the most logical to follow—the most curious to me is the general feeling in the modern dance that nineteenth-century forms stemming from earlier pre-classical forms are the only formal actions advisable, or even possible to take. This seems a flat contradiction of the modern dance—agreeing with the thought of discovering new or allegedly new movement for contemporary reasons, the using of psychology as a tremendous elastic basis for content, and wishing to be expressive of the "times" (although how can one be expressive of anything else)—but not feeling the need for a different basis upon which to put this expression, in fact being mainly content to indicate that either the old forms are good enough, or further that the old forms are the only possible forms. These consist mainly of theme and variation, and associated devices—repetition, inversion, development, and manipulation. There is also a tendency to imply a crisis to which one goes and then in some way retreats from. Now I can't see that crisis any longer means a climax, unless we are willing to grant that every breath of wind has a climax (which I am), but then that obliterates climax, being a surfeit of such. And since our lives, both by nature by the newspapers, are so full of crisis that one is no longer aware of it, then it is clear that life goes on regardless, and further that each thing can be and is separate from each other, viz: the continuity of the newspaper headlines. Climax is for those who are swept by New Year's Eve.

More freeing into space that the theme and manipulation "holdup" would be formal structure based on time. Now time can be an awful lot of bother with the ordinary pinchpenny counting that has to go on with it, but if one can think of the structure as a space of time in which anything can happen in any sequence of movement event, and any length of stillness can take the place, then the counting is an aid towards freedom, rather than a discipline towards mechanization. A use of time-structure also frees the music into space, making the connection between the dance and the music one of individual autonomy connected at structural points. The result is the dance is free to act as it chooses, as is the music. The music doesn't have to work itself to death to underline the dance, or the dance create havoc in trying to be as flashy as the music.

For me, it seems enough that dancing is a spiritual exercise in physical form, and that what is seen, is what it is. And I do not believe it is possible to be "too simple." What the dancer does is the most realistic of all possible things, and to pretend that a man standing on a hill could be doing everything except just standing is simple divorce—divorce from life, from the sun coming up and going down, from clouds in front of the sun, from the rain that comes from the clouds and sends you into the drugstore for a cup of coffee, from each thing that succeeds each thing. Dancing is a visible action of life.

Merce Cunningham

Four Events That Have Led to Large Discoveries, 1994

During the course of working in dance, there have been four events that have led to large discoveries in my work.

The first came with my initial work with John Cage, early solos, when we began to separate the music and the dance. This was in the late forties. Using at that time what Cage called a "rhythmic structure"—the time lengths that were agreed upon as beginning and ending structure points between the music and the dance—we worked separately on the choreography and the musical composition. This allowed the music and the dance to have an independence between the structure points. From the beginning, working in this manner gave me a feeling of freedom for the dance, not a dependence upon the note-by-note procedure with which I had been used to working. I had a clear sense of both clarity and interdependence between the dance and the music.

The second event was when I began to use chance operations in the choreography, in the fifties. My use of chance procedures is related explicitly to the choreography. I have utilized a number of different chance operations, but in principle it involves working out a large number of dance phrases, each separately, then applying chance to discover the continuity—what phrase follows what phrase, how time-wise and rhythmically the particular movement operates, how many and which dancers might be involved with it, and where it is in the space and how divided. It led, and continues to lead, to new discoveries as to how to get from one movement to the next, presenting almost constantly situations in which the imagination is challenged. I continue to utilize chance operations in my work, finding with each dance new ways of experiencing it.

The third event happened in the seventies with the work we have done with video and film. Camera space presented a challenge. It has clear limits, but it also gives opportunities of working with dance that are not available on the stage. The camera takes a fixed view, but it can be moved. There is the possibility of cutting to a second camera which can change the size of the dancer, which, to my eye, also affects the time, the rhythm of the movement. It also can show dance in a way not always possible on the stage: that is, the use of detail which in the broader context of theater does not appear. Working with video and film also gave me the opportunity to rethink certain technical elements. For example, the speed with which one catches an image on the television made me introduce into our class work different elements concerned with tempos which added a new dimension to our general class work behavior.

The fourth event is the most recent. For the past five years, I have had the use of a dance computer, Life Forms, realized in a joint venture between the Dance and Science departments of Simon Fraser University in British Columbia. One of its uses is as a memory device: that is, a teacher could put into the memory of the computer exercises that are given in class, and these could be looked at by students for clarification. I have a small number of particular exercises we utilize in our class work already in the memory. But my main interest is, as always, in discovery. With the figure, called the Sequence Editor, one can make up movements, put them in the memory, eventually have a phrase of movement. This can be examined from any angle, including overhead, certainly a boon for working with dance and camera. Furthermore, it presents possibilities which were always there, as with photos, which often catch a figure in a shape our eye had never seen. On the computer the timing can be changed to see in slow motion how the body changes from one shape to another. Obviously, it can produce shapes and transitions that are not available on humans, but as happened first with the rhythmic structure, then with the use of chance operations, followed by the use of the camera on film and video and now with the dance computer, I am aware once more of new possibilities with which to work.

My work has always been in process. Finishing a dance has left me with the idea, often slim in the beginning, for the next one. In that way, I do not think of each dance as an object, rather a short stop on the way.

Merce Cunningham

Merce Cunningham in Conversation with Laura Kuhn

*Following series of video stills from
Walkaround Time, 1968*

LAURA KUHN: In our public conversation at the Brooklyn Academy of Music (BAM) this past season, I asked you, given your eclectic background and training, "Why modern dance, as opposed to musical theater, or ballet, or whatever?" And you answered, quite simply, that it was because of your meeting and subsequent work with John Cage, obviously a very "modern" composer. You elaborated by talking about how this relationship afforded particular kinds of opportunities to you as a choreographer, having to do both with Cage's particular ways of thinking and working, and with the proximity this relationship provided you to other modern composers and artists, their ideas and work. This seemed so consistent with something that I find in both you as a person <u>and</u> in your work—your willingness to explore the possibilities inherent in any circumstances in which you find yourself. The possibilities inherent in the "circumstance" of the coming together of Cage and Cunningham were, clearly, quite rich and also quite sustained, for both of you.

So, I thought it might be interesting to talk today about your work with Cage, specifically about what you've previously identified as being "key" collaborative pieces. Taken together, these number some fourteen works and span more than fifty years. What makes each of these works "key"? Another, perhaps simpler way to put that question might be to ask what has led you, and what now leads you, from one thing to another? How <u>do</u> new works evolve?

I realize I've just asked you a handful of questions to which your life's work is really the most eloquent answer. That said, let's begin by talking about the earliest of these key pieces.

Root of an Unfocus, 1944

MERCE CUNNINGHAM: I had made one or two dances, solos, previous to 1944, but one in particular, called <u>Totem Ancestor</u> (1942), for which John composed the music for prepared piano. It was a dance that was, for lack of another word, expressive, so the structure came out of that. It was also a very short dance, I think, two minutes at the most.

LK *And <u>Root of an Unfocus</u> was what? Five minutes?*

MC Five. John and I planned to give a program that spring, and I think <u>Root of an Unfocus</u> is the first dance that I started to work on after that. He suggested that we try to cooperate using what he called rhythmic structure. <u>Root</u>, for example, was made of three sections. Each section was in a different tempo. The whole piece was five minutes, which for me was enormous. We worked out the idea of the structure—that is, each segment had a specific form, like five times five, as its rhythmic structure.

LK *A square-root form.*

MC That's right. And each one of the three parts was different. I think one was ten times ten.

LK *I think it was eight times eight, ten times ten, and six times six.*

MC That sounds right. Ten is the middle one. So then I started to work. The dance was, in a way, about expression. It was about fear—one of the predominant things in my life.

I had not really worked with this kind of structure before, but I would have trouble in the beginning. On the other hand, I began to realize that the structure was there, to which you could adhere or not. It somehow seemed a marvelous freedom. It was both fixed and free, or definite and free at the same time.

The dance, the expression, was basically about somebody who was frightened, so he looks outside. I don't remember exactly the movements, but it is as though there is something attacking him in some way. The second part is confronting this, so to speak. And the third part is really the realization that the fear is in yourself.

LK *It's internal.*

MC Yes. And the dance ends with this poor figure falling and crawling and rising and falling and rising, but all within this structure. This whole way of working seemed like something that fitted my spirit. I suppose because in a dancer's life there's this constant discipline. How you organize your life around the requirements of the dance thing, dance classes. Everything else you do has to be arranged to fit that structure. So this seemed perfectly reasonable to me. Also, I never applied, ever, that idea that comes with A-B-A—that you do the A, then do the B, and then you go back comfortably to the A again. That didn't seem to fit at all to the time in which we live.

LK *It's interesting that it's a suitable musical form from the nineteenth century, but it's not a comfortable literary form, certainly not in the twentieth century, and it's not a comfortable dance form anymore. Music is the only place where you still see that form.*

MC For me it wasn't suitable at all. And John wasn't having anything to do with that.

LK *This was not, though, the first piece that you did with John in which music and dance were independent, was it?*

MC Yes, it was.

LK *Oh, so it really is a seminal piece.*

MC Because in <u>Totem Ancestor</u> he followed my counts, adhered to that. I really think <u>Root of an Unfocus</u> is the first important work, at least for me . . .

LK *. . . where that independence happens.*

MC I found it so simply enlivening, an opening. You had to be strict, but you didn't have to be strict in relationship to the music, note by note. At the end of the structure, of course, each time, we came together. There's one moment in that dance, I think, where one of those extraordinary loud sounds that John put in it, in the piano preparations, comes smack with something I did. I think it was Richard Lippold, the sculptor, who saw the dance, and he said that moment is so astonishing. Because you've not had this, and then when you have it, it's unforgettable.

LK *It's the kind of thing that makes audiences suspicious.*

MC It's as though you fixed it. I like that idea. I don't care whether it's fixed or not, but I like it that it can be both ways.

LK *So this is a piece that begins to pull away from the traditional idea of sharing information about a dance. You're beginning to weaken those threads, so to speak.*

MC I think it's sharing information, but in a separate way, about two separate identities, right from the beginning.

LK *Did John know that the piece was loosely about fear? Would you have talked about that?*

MC I think probably I did. I'm more likely to simply work something out than I am to talk, but I'm sure that I did.

Sixteen Dances for Soloist and Company of Three, 1951

LK *Was this in fact the first piece wherein you used chance?*

MC Yes, on a very minimal scale. There were two chance operations in it. The idea of the dance comes from the Indian classical theater of the permanent emotions. Four light, and four dark, and tranquility, which should pervade all. It's such a marvelous idea about theater, I think. It's amazing. It immediately makes it less personal, for me, right from the top. The idea of tranquility.

Anyway, I arranged mine in the form of a prelude, then one of the emotions, a prelude, an emotion, and so on. The last thing was tranquility. It was something like dark, light, dark, light, dark—like Anger . . . prelude, emotion, prelude, emotion, prelude, emotion, prelude, emotion. That's eight. Repeat: that's sixteen. I gave this structure to John, so he could compose. It was for a small orchestra.

It lasted—for me it was an enormous work—almost fifty minutes, I think. But I very carefully figured the time, using minutes now. By this time we weren't any longer thinking about metronomic speeds at all, simply lengths of time. The preludes were anything from half a minute to a minute. The dances were two to four minutes.

LK *His piece uses sixty-four different sounds, eight of which get replaced each time, so that by the end there's a completely new "instrumentation" in terms of sounds. Was your piece like that? How was your piece structured?*

MC I did it in time, really, with the idea that there would be a prelude, and then something about fear, and then a prelude, and something about humor, all the way through. But I made the length of each one different. I was very conscious of that.

LK *The "Erotic" is a duet, as I recall.*

MC Yes. And "Humor." I called it "The Odious Warrior," a warrior battling away in that incredible costume I had.

LK *You did all the solos. Who was with you for the duets?*

24

1. The Events, first begun in 1964, are performances made up of elements from the repertory and new material developed especially for the particular Event. Each involves the entire company, is arranged specifically for the space it will occupy, is presented without intermission, and allows for the possibility of several independent activities happening at the same time.

MC Dorothy Berea, Anneliese Widman, and Mili Churchill. They came from other techniques, primarily the Graham work then. And it really was the time I realized I couldn't work with either ballet dancers or modern dancers that way. I had to really train them myself, or not do it. Just give the whole thing up.

LK *I interrupted you before, about chance. You said you used chance in two very tiny ways.*

MC One came at the end, about the order of the last eight, maybe. I thought I could decide, but I could just as easily—with this principle of light and dark—toss a coin.

LK *So you made a decision—I think an important decision, based on the work that follows—that the order wasn't necessary, any given order.*

MC That I didn't have to choose it, as long as I stayed within the structure.

LK *You had decided prelude, dark, interlude, light, interlude, or whatever. But what dark, what light, that didn't matter.*

MC Yes, exactly. And then there was one section, I think it was one of the interludes, where all four of us were in this. I made charts—very small, very simple things. I mean now they're simple, but they were so unbelievably complicated.

LK *It was like John tossing dice for six weeks to compose a piece.*

MC These three women were just hustling beyond belief. They really had trouble and they were unhappy. Except one. Sometime after the first performance we were doing it again, and I had to replace one of the dancers. There was a dancer who had been with Graham—but she'd also studied with me—named Joan Skinner, who asked me if she could be in this. I knew her dancing was very good. She loved the whole experience. She said it was so freeing. I think it must have taken months to make that piece. For me it was incredibly long.

LK *Well, that was an evening-length work. At the time, it was not uncommon, was it, to have a dance concert last fifty minutes? Or is that too short?*

MC No, but I think we had an intermission when we did it, so that would make the whole evening an hour or so. Anyway, it was so odd, regardless.

LK *This piece has made a comeback, you know. It was done by a Butoh troupe out in California.*

MC Oh, I know, and I thought John's score was very beautiful. So interesting, if you listen to how it changes through the course of the work.

LK *It had a lot of odd percussion, didn't it?*

MC Yes. Beautiful gongs in the last dance. There was a big festival at some Broadway theater, and we were included with this work. They were scared to death, of course, because it was Martha Graham, Doris Humphrey, José Limón, and others whose work was more known to the public. They didn't want me to do the whole piece. And I said I wouldn't do it otherwise. So we did it straight through, without an intermission, which was phenomenal for us. The reception was, shall we say, mixed. And the orchestra. . . . They had this thing with water for the gongs, you know? The gongs dipped in water? Well, they were union musicians, or the crew couldn't think of this. Nobody would fill the bucket, so I can still see John carrying the water.

LK *You don't do this piece now, do you? Are there parts of it in Events[1]?*

MC No. I don't have any of it. There was no way for me to write everything down. It was simply hopeless. I didn't think that way, anyway, then.

LK *Which may be why other dance companies feel comfortable in doing things with Cage's Sixteen Dances, because your work is not alive in the repertory.*

MC Yes, I'm glad they use the music, though. I think it's wonderful.

Suite for Five in Space and Time, 1956

LK *The next on this list of important pieces for you and John is* Suite for Five in Space and Time *(although "in Space and Time" was dropped from the title subsequently), and in that piece, like John in his piece for* Suite for Five, *you used imperfections on paper to dictate how you worked.*

MC Yes, that was for the space. It was originally a suite of solos for myself because John and I were doing solo programs in 1951 and 1952.

LK *There was a piece called* Solo . . .

MC Solo Suite in Space and Time. There were five solos and the space was arranged with the imperfections—one piece of paper for each solo. I numbered the imperfections by chance as to what was one, so that again, instead of my mind saying, "Oh, I could go from here to here," I was confronted with something where I had to go in a way I didn't know about. And I wrote the movements down.

LK *This was five years later, after* Sixteen Dances?

MC No, the Solos were made in 1952, 1953. Each of the five were in a different tempo. But I was beginning to lose that thing about tempo more and more, because I could see no reason why I couldn't do a fast movement and then a slow movement. And the music, of course, was the Music for Piano (4–84).

LK *With a great deal of silence.*

MC Yes. John picked particular ones for all the solos, and eventually there came to be a trio, a quintet, a solo for Carolyn Brown, and a duet for Carolyn and myself. For the duet, you take a piece of paper and mark the imperfections. Then you would superimpose the papers to see where they might meet or not. And then working with the movements, which I'd figured out and written down somehow.

LK *This must have been fun for you, but also, as you said, liberating.*

MC Also difficult. I would look and say, "Isn't that amazing!" Or something would come up and I'd think, "Well, what can I do with that?" But if you tried it, something else would happen. And so over four years, probably, we had the whole suite.

LK *Where you'd added a trio, you added a quartet, and you added a duet, I think. And there was supposed to be a sextet, but Bruce King couldn't make the rehearsals, or something.*

MC That's right, so I dropped that. And also I put in a solo for Carolyn. We did it for years. And sometimes there would be two pianos. If, say, we were in a situation where two were available, John and David [Tudor] could both play. David would play something else from the Music for Piano (4–84). It would be marvelously enriched. But the problem was—with the dancers, of course—we had begun to hear, with only John playing, certain things as cues.

LK *It's the beginning of the end with this piece, isn't it? The idea of cues.*

MC Yes. I remember Carolyn saying, "We missed something."

LK *The other thing about this piece, which I think is important and relevant to your more recent work, is the fact that this work was made to be seen from four sides.*

MC Well, if you're looking at a piece of paper, you can turn it around, and you have four sides.

26

LK *So it suggested that you could have four exit points, four entrance points. And also significant is the fact that meter was abandoned.*

MC It simply had to do with how you proportioned things within different lengths of time.

LK *Are the dancers for the first time relying upon internal counting and cues from each other and feeling a rhythm with each other?*

MC I think over a period of time working at something you get a physical, internal sense of how long something takes. You do that in life. How long it takes you to get someplace. That's because you've done it for years.

LK *And you began to trust that in this piece, that it could be done.*

MC We'd begin to rehearse and it kept coming out the same all the time.

LK *You have that now when the dancers rehearse* Ocean *(1994) without sound and they're within a minute over ninety minutes of a piece, consistently.*

MC Oh, yes. Physical proportions, your muscular memory about how something goes.

LK *But most companies would never fathom working like that. Like the New York City Ballet, would they ever contemplate being able to follow an internal rhythm about a piece, from start to finish?*

MC They would. They would trust it and work at it. There's no question that any dancer with sense could do this. It's not as though it's so mysterious. It's just that they're so conditioned. And people always ask, "Well, how can you dance without music?" And I just say, "Well, you walk around the street without music."

LK *Right. You don't count your steps.*

MC You don't have to have that kind of support for that, so why can't you see that that can be extended into any kind of movement?

LK *I think that, in some ways, is one of the most shocking things about your work, for people who are new to it when they see it. They're baffled or delighted, or whatever, but when they actually experience that there are no counts here, they're astonished.*

MC In any familiar sense, yes.

LK *The critical appraisal of this piece was that it was a very classical piece, which is interesting.*

MC Well, in a way, it is. When we redid it, I'm sure it looked that way. Not that the movements are classical, but each shape is so clear.

LK *One thing that we see in John's piece in this, and not in yours yet, is that John was relinquishing control to his players. That he was setting something in motion in his scores that the players actually did. And you have not yet, in the works we have talked about, done that. The work is strictly choreographed, the dancers are doing what it is that they're supposed to be doing. With some leeway, but they're not given a space of time in which they can do something from a gamut, for example, as John was doing.*

MC No. Very early on I tried teaching without count for a technique class. I would give them the exercise and then not count. And from my point of view, I simply gave up, it simply didn't work. There was no clear definition in the physical shape, because they had nothing to pin it to. Now, you could have come at it another way. I don't think that what I did is the only way, by any means. But I realized in order to make a physical shape, some kind of structure is necessary. Now, I myself don't use an accompanist in that sense because I often want to change the time of something. At the same time, as with <u>Suite</u>, each shape had to be clear. Also, even in this one, there are slight variations about how long it takes a given dancer to do this movement, then he or she can speed up the next one so they end at the same time. Now another dancer may take a shorter time with this and longer with this, but the overall thing is that I began to see through the teaching.

LK *And that begins to be a distinguishing thing about your work, those "internal" differences.*

MC Yes. So it had a little bit of that kind of flexibility. But I only tried improvisation once, in a summer workshop someplace. Well, it didn't work for me. I could see it wasn't where my thinking was. I would say, "But you're repeating the same thing!"

LK *Yes, it's the problem with improvisation, isn't it, the reliance upon the known?*

MC Yes, and they would repeat the same shape, in the same space, in the same time. I would say, "Now, couldn't you move the space a little?" Well, no. Anyway, I didn't do that.

LK *Part of what I'm interested in here is what John was doing and what you were doing, and how you bled into each other, and not. In some ways, you said, this won't work here for me, and the dancers. The medium is different, whatever the reasons were.*

MC Also, it seems to me that musicians are more or less stationary and dancers are not. And if the work gets complicated and they don't know exactly where they're going . . .

LK *You have collisions!*

MC We've had a few of those in the normal way of working, and that's bad enough.

Antic Meet, 1958

LK *I was delighted to see <u>Antic Meet</u> on this list of important works, because it's such a cheerful little piece. It's "meet," in the sense of athletic meet, and John's music is the <u>Concert for Piano and Orchestra</u>. And this is clichés of vaudeville, various styles of dancing taking the place of contests.*

MC Yes. There were ten sections, and Bob Rauschenberg did the decors. It was wonderful.

LK *Was that the first piece Bob did decors for?*

MC No, <u>Minutiae</u> (1954) was the first. And then he did <u>Summerspace</u>. Both <u>Summerspace</u> and <u>Antic Meet</u> were on the same summer school program. <u>Antic Meet</u>, oh boy.

LK *Extensive notes for this work exist in the form of the letter that you wrote to Bob telling him what he wanted to know. You were trying to give him some sense of the work. Of course, the work, as it ended up, bears <u>some</u> resemblance, but not a lot.*

MC Not very much, no. I remember when I told him I wanted to do this dance with a chair on my back, he stopped. And he said, "Well, if you have a chair, can I have a door?" I said, "Sure, but we'd need to have a door." And he said, "Oh, any theater has a door." Well, Bob hadn't been in the theater often at that time. And I said, "Bob, I don't think you're going to find it that way." So, he ended up making a door, which was wheeled out and I opened it up and Carolyn came through it. I probably, in that letter or someplace, put the timings. I don't know if I stuck to them.

LK *So, was <u>Antic Meet</u> the first time you and John worked together with just an overall timing?*

MC Yes, it was like thirty minutes, I think. It must have been. It was exact.

LK *But no internal proportions?*

MC No. I proportioned mine, but we were using the <u>Concert for Piano and Orchestra</u>, which could be any length. And then when we toured, there was a version that David made for the piano. Because we couldn't carry an orchestra with us.

LK *But the internal proportions, not to say that they were abandoned, but there was no longer any necessity to bring them together—the music with the dance. We're seeing a kind of progression away from mandatory internal structure between the two of you.*

MC To where it's this: the curtain goes up, the curtain goes down.

LK *That's wonderful. That's very liberating.*

MC That's true, though, because in <u>Suite for Five</u> we had cues, in a way. A given piano sound would tell us something as to where we were. We didn't have to be on the sound, but it was a guidepost. But with <u>Antic Meet</u>, no, it was the dance itself, the length of time.

LK *Have you brought back bits and pieces of it in <u>Events</u>?*

MC No, I don't think so. The trouble is, again, there were no clear notes. There was that tumbling act that Remy Charlip and I did, and those marvelous shirts, you know?

LK *I've seen those photographs, which are really wonderful. This was an audience pleaser. It premiered at the American Dance Festival, right?*

MC Yes, which was then at the Connecticut College School of the Dance. I remember one of the music people there who thought John's music was very good as humorous music.

LK *That must have amused John.*

MC I'll bet. Well, I think John was used to that by then.

<u>Variations V</u>, 1965

LK *The next work on this list of important pieces is <u>Variations V</u>. It's really interesting, Merce, the works that you've pinpointed, because each work in sequence here has had a relationship to the work before it, although <u>Variations V</u> is very different in the sense of all the technology involved, the sort of circus element of it, the simultaneity.*

MC Yes, the synchronicity, if you can call it that. But the principle for all of this was that by the use of microphones or electronics, the dancers and the music people could make sounds also. But the dancers could make sounds which then could be taken by the music people and used later.

John said he would like to use contact microphones. I wasn't very clear about that, I remember. He said, "Oh, it's a contact microphone placed on something and then by some vibration a sound is picked up." So I said, "Well, then, it could be anything." And he said, "Exactly." So we had a plant, which was fake, and you could take the leaves off and rearrange them. Carolyn did that. Each time you did that there was this kind of sound picked up. With one of the dancers, we had two chairs and a table, and we moved the thing on which there were contact microphones. So when you pushed them, or picked them up, or whatever, this kind of scuttle went on. Same thing with the bicycle at the end—it had a contact microphone on the wheels.

LK *So in a very real sense, you and John worked in tandem on this, because John's <u>Variations V</u>, like the <u>Variations</u> series in general, has to do with sound generated by action, whatever that might be.*

MC Yes, by something that produces it. Though it wasn't to produce a sound which you then heard, but which was made available, like a library.

LK *Yes, and that's an extremely important distinction. Because it's interesting to see now, with computer technology being what it is, these theaters with a black box, which is rigged. You have a lot of movement companies experimenting with tripping light, or tripping something that activates sound. And it's always in real time, and it's always literal. So you step over here and it produces a "C" in this sonority, which is not so interesting.*

MC No, you know exactly, "Oh, he's going to do that and there's going to be a sound." Whereas with us, it was a mess.

LK *An interesting mess.*

MC Oh, yes. But Moog, Robert Moog [the sound engineer for music], had never been in the theater before, I don't think.

LK *Or since. You may have killed him off.*

MC He was so fascinated by the dancing that he didn't do any work. We were constantly saying, "Moog, we gotta get to it!" And that was a long work. It was forty-five minutes.

LK *Wasn't there also a film?*

MC There were films by Stan VanDerBeek.

LK *And Nam June Paik mixed them?*

MC I think so. We had wanted closed-circuit television, which Nam June would take and then play later, the same thing like the sound. But it was way beyond the budget. And we, the dancers, all danced over wires. Because the wires ran from the microphones, which were all around the stage, and then they would run to where they could connect with the music. These were all taped down, of course. This is all pre-going-to-the-moon, or whatever, because we couldn't do wireless.

LK *This must have been daunting for you.*

MC Yes, it was terrible. Two sounds were possible: one somewhat like when you approach the supermarket and the door opens—sensors—and there was another one.

LK *As I understand it, there were poles.*

MC Microphone poles. So that the microphones would pick up something. But there were also these photo-electric cells on the floor.

LK *One thing that I think you did in this piece that you hadn't done before, was essentially indeterminate movement. Or, there were indeterminate aspects to the piece, like the ordering of actions.*

MC That's right, they could actually change. I don't remember how. Oh, there was one thing I devised for Barbara Dilley and Gus Solomons. There was an arrangement so she could put a pad on her head, and a contact microphone was underneath in some way. And I had Gus turn her upside down and lift her up and down. So, again, there was a sound possibility, but it was visual. Because the point about those actions is that they should be something that you could look at. And it didn't matter how long they were. So in that sense they were indeterminate. I never made it precise.

LK *But you couldn't control what they did and how long that took.*

MC No, and also in that sense it was indeterminate in the actions.

LK *You haven't, or you didn't, I should say, pursue that. It was a phase in your life as a choreographer. You explored this in a time when others around you were exploring it as well. Clearly John was exploring it, and Stan was exploring it.*

MC I probably didn't because I could see it was possible, obviously, but I just grew more interested in making steps. It's that simple. And I began to see, with each of these pieces, more possibilities about complexity in steps. Not that I could yet give them.

Second Hand, 1970

LK *The next piece is <u>Second Hand</u>. This piece grew out of a suggestion from John that you do two more movements to Erik Satie's <u>Socrate</u>. You had done one movement earlier.*

MC Yes. At that time, the musicians were John, David Tudor, and Gordon Mumma. And both David and Gordon had come to me at some point, before I began on <u>Second Hand</u>, asking if the next piece could <u>not</u> be for electronics because they had a hard enough time doing two setups, and if they had to do three, if each piece required electronics, that was very difficult for them, under our circumstances.

LK *The program had two other pieces, at least one of which had an electronic setup?*

MC Yes, or both. So immediately John said, "Oh, you have to do the <u>Socrate</u>!" He didn't say, "You <u>should</u>." He said, "You <u>have</u> to."

LK *Was he working on that at the time, do you think?*

MC No. Well, he may have been working on the piano reduction, that's possible. But years back he had said, "You have to do the whole thing, sometime." I had made a solo, way back in the 1940s, to the first movement.

LK *That was <u>Idyllic Song</u>?*

MC Yes. So, I said, "All right, I'll do it! I'll do it!" And John said he would make a piano reduction of the <u>Socrate</u> that he could play. He was in Illinois during this period, and he worked on that, and I had a recording, and also a score of <u>Socrate</u>, to make the dance. The first movement was a solo, the second movement was a duet with Carolyn Brown and myself, and the third movement was for the whole company. It was thirty minutes, and I never left the stage.

LK *So this was <u>your</u> piece.*

MC I was beginning to feel at home. So, we were rehearsing to the recording in New York, and periodically I had telephone conversations with John where he would say he was working on this piano reduction. Well, about a month before we were to premiere the work, I think in Brooklyn, at BAM, John phoned to say that the publisher in Paris had refused to give permission for his piano reduction. But he said, "Don't worry. I'll do something." And I said, "Well, all right. I won't worry." So he phoned back again in a day or so and said, "I'm going to make a piano reduction that uses Satie's phraseology and metrical proportions and all of that, the rhythm, but I'm going to use chance methods as to where the notes fall, so that there's no problem with the publisher." So I said, "But there's going to be a problem with us, because we've been rehearsing to the record." He said, "Oh, no, there'll be no problem at all." John, you know. Well, he finally came to New York, before we were to do all this, maybe two weeks. He started to play and, of course, we were all nonplussed. I can still see the looks on the dancers' faces, because they were so accustomed to hearing the Satie, not the phrasing, but the sounds, the melodic thing. John had changed it all. Anyway, we continued. There is, by the way, a marvelous photo in David Vaughan's book of us rehearsing the Satie piece to John's music, and you see John playing the piano. We did it, and presented it, of course, and it's the last piece I ever made to music.

LK *Is that because of the frustration of this experience?*

MC No, no.

LK *This piece is one of the few pieces in which you allow the dancers some freedom, isn't it? In the hands and fingers.*

2. Since 1970, Cunningham has had his studio in the Westbeth building, an artists' housing and studio complex in New York's Greenwich Village. The space on the eleventh floor, which included the former auditorium, has superb views across the Hudson River and of the New York skyline. Over the years, Westbeth has been not only a rehearsal space but also the site for performances and the filming of works such as <u>Locale</u> (1979) and <u>Channels/Inserts</u> (1981).

MC Yes. In the third movement, I gave them certain hand and finger positions—there may have been a dozen—but each dancer was allowed to do whatever one he or she chose to do when he or she chose to do it. It wasn't fixed by me. I often do that in pieces. Not to any extent now, because the works are so complex that if I add that, it's very hard. Simply to do the steps, that's hard enough.

LK *What was the work like in terms of dramatic structure? Did it follow the Satie at all?*

MC I think so. The first movement was a solo, but that was simply made that way. The second is a duet, and in <u>Socrate</u> itself, it's about Socrates and Alcibiades, walking by the riverbank. And the third movement is someone describing the death. In that sense I think the piece pertains to that. I didn't make it descriptive, but it certainly entered into my feelings.

LK *Why <u>Second Hand</u>?*

MC Well, John said he was going to call his <u>Cheap Imitation</u> to just jump ahead of the critics. And I said, "Well, if you call yours <u>Cheap Imitation</u>, I'll call mine <u>Second Hand</u>."

LK *No allusion to <u>Socrate</u> in either of those titles. That piece had no set. Is that right?*

MC I don't think it even had a drop. It had beautiful costumes by Jasper [Johns]. In each the coloring was different, and you didn't realize until the bow, when we all lined up, that they fed one to the other, one color on one side. And when I realized that's what Jasper had done, I arranged the bow so that the edge of the costume of one led into another, as a spectrum, all the way across. It was quite striking.

LK *Were there times in the dance where you noticed things happening with color because of that?*

MC I don't think so.

LK *Is it something that you would notice now? If you put this piece on the stage, and you weren't dancing in it, would you see color connections in the movement?*

MC Oh, no. You might at times, but it wasn't made that way. I think that color can add something of its own, not something that I would decide. What I would like would be sunsets, <u>real</u> sunsets. I see them at Westbeth[2] every day, and they're beautiful.

LK *Now didn't you have that once? You told me about a performance in an outdoor amphitheater, in France maybe, where the back of the theater is open, and you see the sun setting.*

MC Was that in Arles? It could have been. It's marvelous. Light, first of all, is so beautiful, and it changes so continuously. You look, you look away, and you look back, and then you realize it's changed.

<u>Un Jour ou Deux</u>, 1973

LK *I always think of this work, unfairly, as your <u>Sounddance</u> piece, since it gave birth, on your return to New York from Paris, to <u>Sounddance</u>. This was a commission from the Festival d'Automne. You worked with twenty-six dancers from the Paris Opéra?*

MC Yes. All were members of the Paris Opéra Ballet. Most of them had gone to school there, and grown up in that regime. I had three or four <u>étoiles</u>, well three <u>real</u> ones, two <u>soloistes</u>, that's another rank, and then the rest of the balance of the twenty-six were from the corps de ballet.

LK *Was this your longest piece to date? It was ninety minutes.*

MC I think so. I mean, <u>Events</u> had been that long, but each has been made up of different things. I think maybe it is. <u>Sixteen Dances</u> was only forty-five minutes.

LK *Which was long for its time.*

MC Oh, yes. <u>Un Jour ou Deux</u> was to take a whole evening.

LK *Was it for this piece that you were offered either the whole evening or a share of it?*

MC Michel Guy, the sponsor of all this, had founded the Festival d'Automne—he had proposed this project to me, that I come and work with the dancers of the Paris Opéra to make a work. He said, "Would you like to make a work that would be on a program with two other pieces?" I thought and I said, "No." He smiled. He was a marvelous man. Then he said, "Well, would you like to make three pieces for the evening, or would you like it to be a single piece?" I said, "I'd like it to be a single piece." He smiled again. The result was <u>Un Jour ou Deux</u>.

LK *When you do a piece like that—you did a ninety-minute piece, and you worked with the dancers for nine weeks—was the piece complete when you arrived? Was it in hand, so to speak, and then you taught it?*

MC No. I had worked out some sections, or ideas for sections. I didn't have the computer then, for example. And I had written out some phrases, I remember. Oh, no. I slugged it out.

LK *So you were making the work as you were teaching the work.*

MC Every day I had the rehearsal time, and I took the first hour, maybe slightly less, for class. Because although they had their own classes of classic work in the morning, I knew if they didn't know mine forwards and backwards it would never work at all.

LK *So you had three things going on: you were making a piece, you were teaching a piece, and you were training dancers in Cunningham technique.*

MC Yes. And also, in the beginning weeks, in a studio that was extremely small. Anybody in the opera world will know exactly what I'm talking about if I say "Salle C." It was not much bigger than our small studio, with twenty-six people every day. It was difficult. Also it was very difficult for me then to reach them, because I didn't speak French well. I didn't know them, I didn't know anything about the Paris Opéra Ballet, except I knew they were a classical ballet company. And they didn't know anything about me. So the two of us, we were like strangers.

LK *They were nervous, weren't they?*

MC Yes. And also they were in a system—it may have changed by now, I don't know—where they came in as children and they took class every day, year after year. Some of them had been there twenty years. They really get ingrown. I don't blame them. But on the other hand, it's also secure, because they didn't have to pay, they were paid. But the thing is, if you do this, you have to work in the ballet for a number of years. Like paying off student loans.

LK *Or like the army.*

MC Yes, I had some of those in the company, and it was very hard to communicate. What I gave was so alien to them in every way. There was no music, I was doing everything to counts, and some of them, of course, never got it. But some began to realize there was something here. I, fortunately, had two wonderful dancers, Wilfride Piollet and Jean Guizerix, who really helped me so much to make the piece, because they were willing to try, within limits, of course, but try things. Whereas so often with the others. . . . They were very young, some of them, fifteen years old. And it was nine weeks of just daily work.

LK *So that piece was a real challenge for you, because it was so outside of what you were used to. Also for John. He worked with the Paris Opéra Orchestra, yes?*

MC Yes, and I must tell that story.

LK *The piece was Etcetera.*

MC Yes, for three small orchestras.

LK *There were three conductors.*

MC Yes, and the players could move from one of these to the other. And there were these wonderful boxes, which all the players could play, which were cardboard. The French insisted that they be French cardboard. It was very beautiful, that sound. Well, I met John in the hall of the Opéra House, that tomb, after his first rehearsal, his first encounter with the musicians, and I said, "How did it go?" And he said, "Well, when the musicians learned that they had to make up their minds about what notes they might play, they asked for more money."

LK *Did they get it?*

MC Well, Rolf Liebermann, who headed the whole Opéra, solved it all by contriving to pay them as though they were chamber players or something. That was the only way you could get along. John was so upset that he was causing them to pay more money. But Marius Constant, who was one of the conductors, simply said, "Oh, don't worry, they would have asked for it anyway."

LK *Although Un Jour ou Deux has sets by Jasper Johns, Mark [Lancaster] actually realized Jasper's ideas, didn't he? Was that the first time you were working with Mark, in Paris?*

MC Yes. Jasper came at the end. Mark really did all the work. But they got the materials wrong, and they dyed them wrong. And Jasper came and I saw he was working with Mark, and I saw him in the hall in the Opéra, by the costume department, covered with this apron, covered with paint. And I said, "Oh, you look as though you've been here for years." And he said, "Well, I may well be." Oh, boy.

LK *Why is this on the list of important pieces for you and John? I confess to not quite seeing what happened for the two of you, or you.*

MC I suppose that mainly with me it was because I was working with dancers with whom I'd never worked before.

LK *Taking yourself outside of your world.*

MC Totally. I would think even for John, too.

Inlets, 1977

LK *And on to Inlets. This was finally a collaboration with you and John and Morris Graves [stage decors and costumes], whom you both loved. And he, apparently, was supposed to collaborate with you on The Seasons, some thirty years earlier, and dropped out.*

MC Oh, he didn't want to do it. When he heard there was something about the union, Morris said, "No, thank you."

LK *So thirty years forward, fast forward, you finally work with Morris. And in this one, nature, clearly, is key. John's score spells that out, Morris Graves' work, all three of you. The whole idea of nature, the Pacific Northwest, the topography of the Northwest . . .*

MC And also its quiet movement. Now we have Inlets 2. But, in a sense, they're both the same. I used the same material, only I changed the chance.

LK But there's a great deal of stillness in both of those works, a lot of silence, which is also true of Cage's score, <u>Inlets</u>, with the conch shells and the contingency of the players. The sound is so amazing. And you're watching that and it's a very sleepy piece, in the sense that there's just so much silence in it.

MC And also the sound of the water when you hear it, kind of a little lap of sound.

LK I understand that John's original intention, with respect to the fire—because it's the three elements: air, fire, and water—was that he wanted to have a fire live in the theater.

MC Well, we tried it in Seattle, in the rehearsal, with pine cones.

LK Which I can imagine would make a wonderful sound.

MC Yes, a marvelous sound, but it brought out the fire engines because the smoke detectors went off. And the sponsor had to do a great deal of explaining.

LK But that piece is actually interesting for John, in the sense that it was the first time, in a work with you, that he so fully used or created a situation in which the sounds were not of his design. He couldn't control either the quality or the timings of the sounds.

MC Exactly.

LK So, for him, it was very much what we've been talking about, which is a kind of time structure for himself: in thirty minutes you will rock these water-filled shells, and you are necessary to rock them, but what you produce . . .

MC You may not produce any sounds.

LK Yes, but you are very necessary. How was your choreography relative to that? Was there anything about that kind of contingency?

MC It had many different kinds of movement, a great deal of air, and it had to be fixed because of possible disasters, someone leaping and then someone coming in, and all that. To me it was like you might be watching something like an inlet, or something small where there were many different happenings, little animals, or a leaf, or something about a bush, where you couldn't judge it. I had to set it, because of the catastrophe problem, because of accidents.

LK Did you think about making it—and I understand that you made it—so that it had a quality of happenstance, if you will?

MC Yes, and I think I probably also thought of water, quiet. I was thinking of those places when I was a child on Puget Sound. It was very peaceful. It wasn't the ocean, but that kind of quiet thing of a small beach.

LK Where there's so much life that's apparent.

MC Oh, yes.

LK And not violent, the way the East is, in terms of its water. I see this, too, Merce, and maybe this is presumptuous, but it feels a little bit like in the middle of the 1970s—certainly by <u>Inlets</u> and maybe a little bit before, say between <u>Un Jour ou Deux</u> and <u>Inlets</u>— that there is beginning to be a kind of separation between you and Cage. I don't mean an "at odds-ness," but rather that you're both understanding more about your own craft and your own interests within that craft. John was moving very much toward a kind of contingency-based composition, trying to understand the relationship between himself as composer and his players, given that his medium was sound. And you, in a very similar way, were finding your voice as a choreographer and finding what interested you about working with live dancers. And that they didn't necessarily coincide so tidily anymore. But nonetheless, you found ways of working that were very compatible.

MC Well, I think we simply realized that that opening we'd made, of how you connect sound with sight, could broaden more and more. Because if you think of it abstractly, you could have any sound with any sight.

LK *So establishing that way of working, thirty or twenty-five years before* Inlets, *resulted, maybe unconsciously even, in a kind of freedom to really be different. Which, of course, was the premise that you started out with. It continues, and you see that in these few remaining works. I just have one little question for you about* Inlets: *There's been a suggestion about the statuesque poses, those signature poses in that piece, as being related to photographs of Nijinsky. Is that true?*

MC I didn't think of it. This happens in every situation. The body is limited in certain ways. You take a position, and anybody can find a reference someplace. I don't think it's wrong, I just think it's the way it is. Let's say the Nijinsky one, where he's sitting with his leg crossed. If you sit in that position, somebody says, "Oh, you're taking it from Nijinsky." But what you maybe have done is you wanted to sit down and stretch your leg and you have . . .

LK *. . . managed to look like Nijinsky when you did it.*

MC I think that happens in all the pieces. In all dances, anyway.

LK *But there have been really literary correlates to some of the works, earlier and later. I'm trying to think, what is the piece with the Dostoyevski epigraph?*

MC Oh, Antic Meet.

LK *Exactly. So, in some of your works, there is a very direct correlation between literary works, or images, that are a kick-off point perhaps, or even more than that.*

MC Yes, like the quote "the absurd is necessary in life." Like a pratfall, and you take off from that.

Trails, 1982

LK *In* Trails, *the next work, you have the idea of two dancers dancing two completely independent things and bringing them together. Which, in a funny way, is like you and John in your earlier pieces.*

MC Well, that's to do with steps, since that's where my mind goes. I kept wondering if there weren't ways that a man dancing with a woman didn't have to stand there just to support her. Was there something that he could do, still with the idea that he could support her, but not be static? And so I thought, well, the only way to do it is to see if you could make phrases that were completely independent, and then put them together and see what happens.

LK *And when you did put them together?*

MC If I saw ways for the guy to touch or lift the lady, I would use it, but at the same time keeping the principle that they're doing separate phrases.

LK *And that piece, also in a curious way, is like the piece John did for it,* Instances of Silence. *That collage of so many different things, even incorporating sounds from here, Sixth Avenue, and from Puerto Rico.*

MC Yes, in the Puerto Rican sounds, one of them was the window shade in my room. But I think you begin to realize, as John did, certainly, that you have this situation where any sound could be utilized and, okay, here I am in this situation, what are the sounds that I could tape or take? I remember the hassle to get that taped.

Roaratorio, 1983

LK *And on to* Roaratorio, *which is very fitting, since we just heard* Roaratorio *in Belfast. That was a piece that was conceived as a radio piece by John in 1979, as a commission from the Westdentscher Rundfunk, Köln (WDR), an hourlong work for radio that you didn't actually see or hear until 1982. Is that right?*

MC In Toronto. That was the first time I heard it.

LK *And was that when the idea to make a dance came, when you finally heard it, or had you talked about that?*

MC No, John proposed it at some point. I think he simply said, "If we keep doing Roaratorio" (and I'm not quoting him), "I hope sometime that you could make something to go with it." And I said, "Oh, I would like that very much." And, of course, there was no possibility up to that time. I went to Toronto to hear it, then, partially because I just wanted to hear it, but partially with the idea that maybe I could think of it that way, even if nothing specific came up.

LK *That piece is a very layered work. It's got collected sounds from Ireland and also from around the world, it's got live musicians, Seamus Heaney and Mel Mercier and Paedar Mercier, many of whom are now long gone. It's got John reading his own poetic text derived from Joyce's* Finnegans Wake. *I may be confused about this, but didn't you and John go to Ireland and collect sounds together?*

MC No, he went with John Fullemann.

LK *But didn't the two of you take a vacation to Ireland?*

MC Oh, yes, but we didn't collect sounds. We just went to look.

LK *And your original work for* Roaratorio—*and I ask because I heard you say this just recently to someone in Belfast*—*which has not been mounted since, was based on jigs and reels and Irish traditional dances, which you then adapted?*

MC Yes, I went to the Performing Arts Library and looked up Irish jigs, and I think somebody gave me a book about them.

LK *And you talked to Seamus, I think, also.*

MC Yes. And it's not that I knew a lot about them, they're much more complicated than my experience with them, but I began to understand something about the sixes and the twos and all of that, and to think in that way. And it wasn't by any means just that. There were all kinds of other things.

LK *Right, but it was touched by that.*

MC Also my visual idea was that this went on for an hour, and it was really out of Finnegans Wake, which is, in a way, like a grand voyage. So I wanted some way for the dancers—I don't know, we must have made exits—but some way that we could be onstage all the time, and gradually move. We started here, if this is the audience, and we gradually moved over to here. Mark [Lancaster] did the clothes, and I said we needed some kind of thing that we could sit on.

LK *There were stools that moved, weren't there?*

MC Well, he did the stools, he found marvelous stools. I said something we could also carry, you know, move ourselves. So that by the end of the piece it's transversed over to here. So we came in here, in the beginning, and all this goes on and the whole thing's moving.

LK *So, again, a literary correlate. The idea of* Finnegans Wake *as a journey.*

MC Spatially, yes. It could be seen as that.

LK *What you said in Belfast interested me very much. You responded to someone who had heard the installation of* <u>Roaratorio</u> *in Belfast, who then said, "Will you ever bring it back, Merce, so that we can have it again as a live piece?" And you said, "I don't know, but if I did, I would do the piece over." Is this something that interests you?*

MC I'd have to think about it.

LK *I love John's piece so much, and I was never privileged enough to see it with your dance.*

MC It was a marvelous piece. We did it in Brooklyn, and the whole thing was wonderful.

<u>Points in Space</u>, 1986

LK *I think of* <u>Points in Space</u> *as the opening of your "postmodern" period, that period everybody likes to talk about. I love the Albert Einstein quote "There are no fixed points in space," which you like very much. This work was originally made for video.*

MC Yes, the BBC.

LK *And the whole idea of no fixed points in space is so in keeping with video, obviously, with multiple viewpoints.*

MC Yes. I think that's one of the great troubles with dance people who use the technology. They don't think that way, for dance. And it's a marvelous way to think.

LK *And this was also the first film work for your company that you actually appeared in, isn't it?*

MC I think you're right. It has Bill Anastasi's set. The BBC studio is a huge, great big thing, seventy-five-by-seventy-five feet, with cameras at this end. And the cameras can move all the way around with cranes. I asked Bill if he would do something for this, and then I saw the space and I thought, "My God! Maybe he could make a drop that went on three sides." Which he did, and it was very beautiful.

LK *Yes, we just saw a bit of it out at BAM this last season. These gorgeous, big color washes.*

MC It looked stunning. The platform was here, and there was space, so the drop began like that. So the cameras could move, they never went back there, but they could come here. And visually I thought that way really was marvelous. Working in television with dancing is very difficult. It's maddening.

LK *Because there are so many possibilities?*

MC Yes, and also you do an angle that you think works, and you realize you've got to change it all because somebody's arm is out [of the camera's "eye"]. I don't mind that, that's part of what it is. Basically I don't object to thinking that way because you're in a different medium.

LK *But you had not had a great deal of experience.*

MC Well, not on that scale, with Elliot [Caplan]. There was also a great problem about the music, John's <u>Voiceless Essay</u>. I went to the studio when they were working downtown.

LK *At Synaesthetics, with Victor Frieburg.*

MC I thought the sound was amazing. But then, of course, the BBC people were . . .

LK *Horrified?*

MC Yes, and they wanted to change it some way. And John simply said, "Well, you may change it but you may not use my name." And that they didn't like very well. But they finally consented. And, of course, John was right.

LK *It's a stunning composition.*

MC Oh, yes. And the thing between the two, on television, is so marvelous. The television people don't ever seem to get that. They always go back to this sentimental music.

LK *Yes, the idea of one thing supporting another thing.*

MC Yes, and awful choices of music. If they got composers who know how to deal with this, the whole musical thing would pick up enormously.

LK *I suppose they have a limited idea about the impact of sound. It's a ludicrous idea, but if you were to take the dance Points in Space and put it to Rachmaninoff, it would alter the piece so drastically that it wouldn't even be recognizable anymore.*

MC And that Stephen Hawking program, when they're talking about outer space, they have this spook music. Whereas some kind of sound that was electronic just by itself would've elaborated the whole thing. But their minds don't work that way. It was a very difficult experience making it. Not that the BBC people weren't wonderful.

LK *It doesn't look it. It looks so beautiful and finished and perfect.*

MC Hard to do, for all of us. First of all, you have to scale with the television camera, which is okay. Then I would make something and think it was going to work on the camera. Then I'd see it on camera and realize it didn't work. I'd been doing this, of course, for several years in our studio, but this was a big number.

LK *So you were making constant alterations?*

MC I'd have to look, and we would often have to do it the day of the shooting. Of course, everybody always has to do this.

LK *How long were you in the studio?*

MC I can't remember. Maybe a week. They were wonderful. Bob Lockyer there is a marvelous man. And I think it's been shown several times, apparently, over the BBC.

Inventions, 1989

LK *Now Inventions is not so long beyond Points in Space. This is a work for the full company, but you didn't dance in it. Only seven dancers appeared at any given time on the stage. You've described the structure as being comprised of sixty-four separate phrases, the continuity is arranged by chance, with further chance possibilities of inventions or additions added to any single phrase. So how did that work, when you say the possibility of additions or inventions?*

MC Well, if something came up, say, where two dancers were doing separate phrases on the stage at the same time and there was some kind of thing where they might approach each other, something else could happen at that moment. I would not have seen that possibility until they did this.

LK *So, do you mean from one performance to the next?*

MC No, no, no. It had to be fixed.

LK *Okay, so it was from rehearsal to performance.*

MC Right. By making sixty-four very separate phrases and, say, in my chance operation it comes up that this person has this one, and at the same time this person has to do this one, then it may turn out that they could . . .

LK *I see. So you started with a plan, which was flexible in its execution.*

MC Yes. I don't remember where it was first given. I remember we did it in Arles, out of doors. The sound was just marvelous.

LK *That was the Sculptures musicales.*

MC Very sharp sounds that come in . . .

2. Merce Cunningham has been using the 3-D human figure animation software, Life Forms® by Credo Interactive, to make new dances since December 1989. Envisioned and developed as a creative tool for choreographers at the Computer Graphics Multi-Media Research Lab at Simon Fraser University in British Columbia, it provides an interactive, graphical interface that enables a choreographer to sketch out movement ideas in space and time.

LK . . . and then disappear.

MC They die away of their own accord. And there's this silence, this stillness, and we're going on.

LK *Yes, we're seeing more of this in John's work. In* Points in Space, *there are huge amounts of silence. You almost forget as you're watching the dance that there is sound. Then all of a sudden you have John hissing or something. And you say, "Oh, yes, there's this score." The same thing a little bit with* Sculptures musicales, *although not so much silence and the sounds are more penetrating.*

MC And abrupt. They start so abruptly.

LK *But then they die away, and there's all this space afterwards.*

MC Yes, and they die away at different lengths. That was beautiful.

LK *That's the Duchamp connection, the Duchamp idea. That was with costumes and decors by Carl Kielblock. He was brought to you by Bill and Dove Bradshaw. Was that his only work with you?*

MC No. Oh, dear, I can't remember, but I know he's done two.

Beach Birds, 1991

LK Beach Birds *has the distinction of being the last work that you did with John. And John never actually saw* Beach Birds. *Or did he?*

MC Yes, he saw it.

LK *That work took its idea from Joyce's projected next work, that wonderful quote "Between the river and the ocean, beach birds." Was that the first work that you did that involved Life Forms[2]? I mean, the first work with John that you did that involved Life Forms?*

MC Yes, but Life Forms goes all the way back to Trackers, actually. That was the first one, but I used it very little, of course.

LK *Which you began work on in 1989?*

MC I think so. In this one, a great deal of the material was put into Life Forms. I really had three images in mind: one was, of course, birds. The other was people on the water. And the third was the way stones, or even sand, take shapes.

LK *The way so-called inanimate objects move?*

MC Yes. So in Beach Birds, where the dancers make those clumps of movement, I think that must come from that. I remember beaches in the West, where you'd have sand dunes piled up that way.

LK *I know we can't talk about Life Forms. That's a whole, huge conversation unto itself. But John really led you to computers, didn't he? He was using computers long before you were, but then you so quickly eclipsed him in terms of your own facility. He used them in a very sophisticated way, but he really didn't have a clue about how that would happen. He had other people, Andrew [Culver] and me, to help him. And he was always so amazed that you actually could do this, and that you didn't have any help.*

MC Well, I had Thecla [Schiphorst].

LK *That's true, but Thecla was in Canada most of the time. And you muddled through. I remember him sending me to your studio one day to see what you were doing. Now that I know you better, I realize what an honor that was, that you actually let me into your studio in the afternoon for an hour.*

MC I figured with the computer, okay, I'd make mistakes, but what

40

difference does it make? In a sense, nothing was a mistake because each time you did something you'd say, "Oh, I never saw that!" So it wasn't a mistake. And then Thecla would come and help me. She'd want to know what I'd done, and I'd show her. And every once in awhile she'd say, "How'd you do that?"

LK *So you'd discover something.*

MC Yes. And she would take it back. So it was a sharing, though her part was bigger than mine. Anyway, with Beach Birds . . . you know, with Life Forms, you could make a kind of fluid look; it may not look that way, but you can see something about the arm going . . .

LK *And that is a characteristic of Beach Birds, the fluidity.*

MC I could do those things. I mean, I could do them myself. But how to pass them to the dancers with the same kind of fluid look. Because it ends up, "Is your elbow bent?" And then they do this, and so it loses all its life. But by putting it in the computer, I could go back and look at it again to catch the original sense.

LK *And the computer image itself suggested to you how the movement was being executed.*

MC Yes, and how to keep this fluidity so you wouldn't lose what it was originally. I like that, both in Life Forms on the Silicon Graphics machine and on the Powerbook.

LK *One of the things that makes Beach Birds such a popular piece is clearly that movement, there's no question. The evocative nature of the movement with respect to the elements you were talking about—birds, and people, and sand objects, sand movement. Also Marsha Skinner's costumes, which are so beautiful. They're just perfect for that piece. And that piece has that gorgeous score by Cage, Four[3], which continues to be one of the most popular of his "number" pieces.*

MC Oh, really?

LK *Yes, because it's so quiet. Kevin Volans recently said that one of his latest compositions, Untitled, from 1997, was absolutely inspired by that piece, because of the placid character of it.*

MC Well, John said there were four things: one was the piano . . .

LK *Or pianos . . .*

MC Yes, and the rainsticks, and the oscillator, and silence. I always say that, because I think it's so evocative about the way he thought of sound.

LK *Yes, because silence is not silence but something else, some other palpable thing.*

Ocean, 1994

LK *I think of Ocean, our last work, as the grown-up Beach Birds, in a way.*

MC Bigger. More birds and they got bigger.

LK *That piece almost warrants a conversation in and of itself. It's so . . . well, it seems to me a couple of things, Merce. John's death in 1992, as difficult as that was, seems also a kind of liberation. In my mind, there's a very clear kind of demarcation of the works after John's death versus the works before, which is nonetheless foreshadowed in Trackers and Change of Address (1992), for example, which are in the 1989– 1991 group. But in Ocean, it seems there is an unabashed move toward the romantic, toward the lavish, toward the loving. It has a kind of sweetness about it.*

MC Well, I don't know. I'm sure that's all possible. When John and I talked about Ocean, I keep remembering what he said. He kept saying he didn't think he could do it.

LK *Why?*

MC His strength was going, so I didn't push it. But we did talk about it, about the whole. And

I loved the idea, in the round. He explained very much about what he wanted in the sound. And he wanted David Tudor involved, and he did mention the underwater sounds, I remember.

LK *And the one hundred twelve musicians, I remember, and the placement of people and things in the space.*

MC Yes, all of that. And then, of course, he went much further with Andy [Culver].

LK *Do you think that John would like <u>Ocean</u>, the way it ended up?*

MC Yes.

LK *So it feels consistent with what you had talked about?*

MC It does. I think because it is such a big piece, and we have to do it in these circumstances so that there are all kinds of unknowns, like how is it going to sound? And you don't have much chance to radically change that. I must say the orchestral sound in this one, in Belfast, was beautiful.

LK *They've all been quite distinct, haven't they? All the performances have been quite unique.*

MC I think on the whole he would like it, but he might question some of the things Andy's done.

LK *They might not have been what John would have done.*

MC No, but that's okay. I think the fact that we continue to do it is an enormous kind of tribute, in a way, to John, because of the idea, because it's so immense, and we're still doing it. We have these possibilities again.

LK *You're doing it twice next year, in Montpellier, France, and in Japan.*

MC I think John would be pleased about Japan, very much.

LK *But just with respect to the movement, though . . . the whole idea of dancing in curved space, as opposed to flat angles. I think it's just so radical. And I don't mean radical like an idea, I mean radical in the sense of what it did to your choreography, what it did to the way you think about choreography.*

MC It was wonderful, and absolutely maddening. What you have to do is every single moment ask, "Where are you?" Every single inch of the step, "Where are you?" "Which way do you face?" It brings up this whole technical thing, it brings up this curving. I remember that day with Jeannie [Steele] and Tom [Caley], and that duet they do in the beginning. They were so ravishing.

LK *Is this where she's dancing around him, and they're doing things out of sync with each other?*

MC Yes. And I kept saying, "Now you have to curve more." And I thought, "Oh, that's what he meant, about curvature of space." Just go a little further, so that flatness disappears. With every single moment of that piece I was trying to check that, to see what was possible, or what I found was possible.

LK *We've now seen this piece in five locales, and the experience in Belfast, my experience and that of others that I talked to, was that the piece was finally settling. That the dancers, in fact (and it may be what you're talking about) are now beginning to dance in curved space. That they're actually beginning to feel a normalcy about it.*

MC I think so. I see it in some, I don't see it in all of them. I must say, for a project like that, there are only about three or four people who have changed since we first did it, which isn't too bad, considering.

LK *I've often wondered, how do you go on from <u>Ocean</u>? How do you go back to a proscenium stage, with right angles, with a front and a back?*

42

MC Well, <u>Ground Level Overlay</u> (1995), which comes after, holds some of that. The very nature of the proscenium stage flattens things out, naturally, and I just take that.

LK *Do you want to make another round piece?*

MC Oh, of course. If I have the chance I would do it, of course. But we're not going to have that, one can't expect to have that, because of the nature of our company's situation. The reason we did <u>Events</u> was we couldn't do three pieces, so what do you do? And John said, "Well, just put things together, and we'll put the music around, and all that." Like a different kind of idea about theater. Not that we thought about it that way, but . . .

LK *So we go right back to my opening comments, that it's really a characteristic of yours, and of John's as well, to see what's possible in the circumstances.*

MC Yes. Instead of saying no, you say yes. I think, on the whole, that's a better way to be because it's brought up all kinds of possibilities of functioning with our work, even though sometimes it was difficult and uncomfortable. The stage in Pittsburgh, for example, was too narrow for <u>Ground Level Overlay</u>.

LK *But you did it.*

MC Oh, yes. I'm sure the public could see that it was too narrow. But it was deep. Okay, but you always deal with that in the theater, in a small way or a big way. And as my works have gotten bigger, then we have to go and do it in some small space.

LK *Does an adaptation—for example, doing <u>Ground Level Overlay</u> in a theater that is too narrow—lead you to anything other than an awareness that you can adapt?*

MC Yes. Two or three years ago we were invited to the American Dance Festival, which has a very small stage, to do a new work. I thought, "Well, I'll make a work for only seven people, and have A and B groups, seven people, and seven people who can alternate." Only I didn't want to do that, really, but I just thought that was a way to take care of that little stage. But then I thought, "I'll just make a piece with all of them and put it in this small space." Okay: <u>CRWDSPCR</u> (1993).

LK *Amazing.*

MC Because that's exactly what it was. You make a plan about something, and then the enemy does something else, and you say, "They're not doing what they're supposed to do!" And, in the meantime, they're battering you to pieces.

LK *You're dead.*

MC Yes. So, you think, "Okay, what can we do?"

LK *So being quick on your feet, no pun intended. One of the things that makes your work so inspiring to people, beyond the dance values of it, is the kind of life qualities that are suggested in it. For example, the adaptation to space.*

MC I think that's what art can do. It can fulfill us in a way—give us something we know is there but don't get to see or experience very often.

LK *I think it was John quoting John Rahn, the editor of <u>Perspectives of New Music</u> in Seattle, who once said that "art can be a practice zone for living." I've always thought that was a very beautiful way of putting it.*

MC Oh, that's wonderful.

<u>Minutiae</u>, 1954 Carolyn Brown in performance, with set by Robert Rauschenberg Photo: John G. Ross

Antic Meet, 1958   Merce Cunningham Dance Company in performance, with costumes by Robert Rauschenberg   Photos, top: Jack Mitchell; bottom: Fannie Helen Melcer

Summerspace, 1958
top: Merce Cunningham in rehearsal, with set by Robert Rauschenberg
Photo: Jack Vartoogian
inset: Merce Cunningham Summerspace (Movement Charts for Six Dancers)
1958 · six sheets; ink on paper Courtesy Barbara Schwartz, New York
bottom: Viola Farber (left) and Carolyn Brown Photo: Richard Rutledge

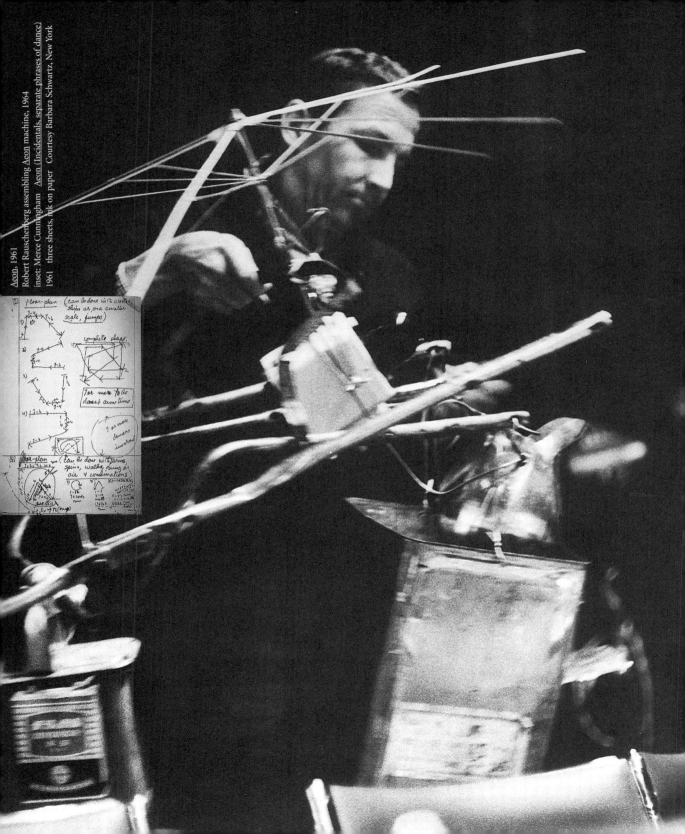

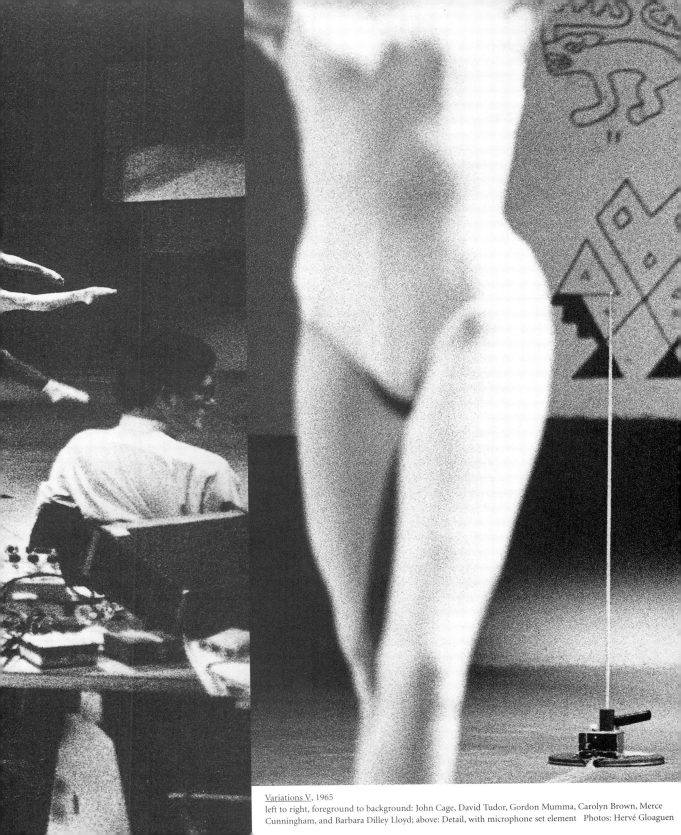

Variations V, 1965
left to right, foreground to background: John Cage, David Tudor, Gordon Mumma, Carolyn Brown, Merce
Cunningham, and Barbara Dilley Lloyd; above: Detail, with microphone set element   Photos: Hervé Gloaguen

Walkaround Time, 1968
left: Merce Cunningham in performance, with decor after Marcel Duchamp's Large Glass (1915–1923), supervised by Jasper Johns
Photo: James Klosty
center: Marcel Duchamp at first performance Photo: Oscar Bailey
right: Video sequence of Cunningham in performance

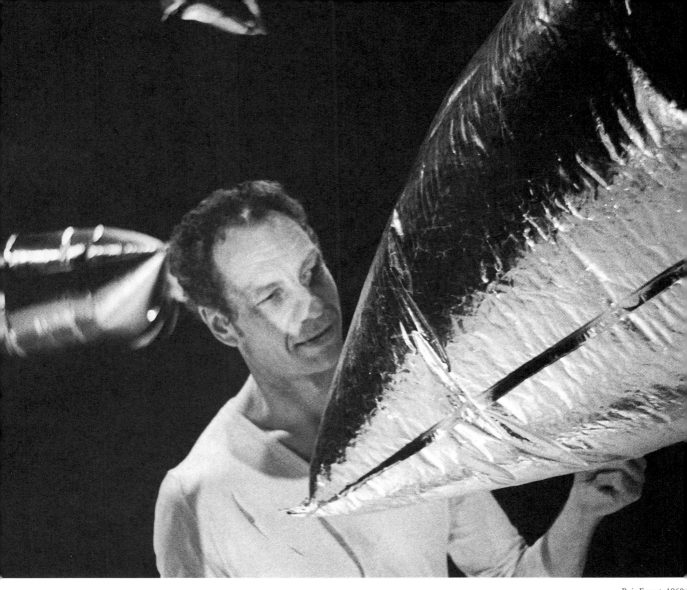

RainForest, 1968
top left: Merce Cunningham with Andy Warhol's <u>Silver Clouds</u> set, 1968; top right: Jasper Johns working on set   Photos: Oscar Bailey
bottom: Carolyn Brown and Chase Robinson in performance, 1968   Photo: James Klosty

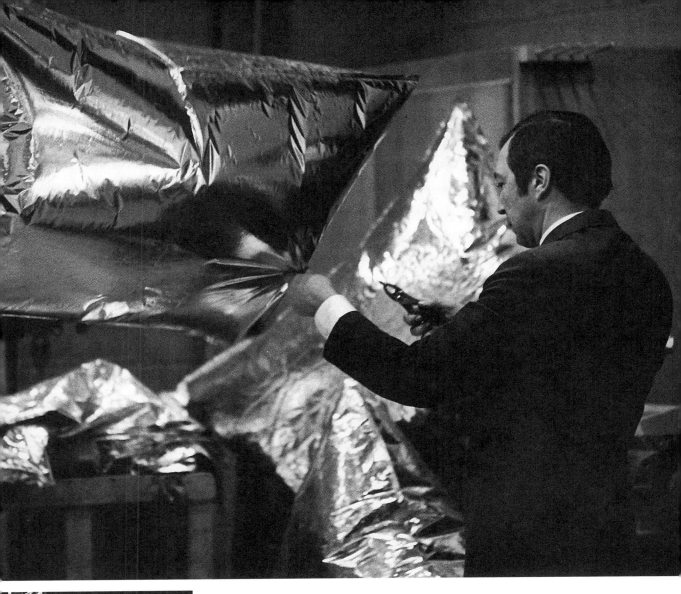

the light walls are placed end to end making a 16 foot light wall
shining offstage from the edge of the dance area either right or left
stage or up or down stage and are then slowly moved across the stage
during the dance - the dance proceedes in the semi - dark - until half
through the dance the light wall is halfway across the stage and the
dancers have been pushed ahead of it and now move a s a group to the
other side - the light side - of the wall and the wall moves across
the stage until it reaches the other side at the end of the dance.

~~I expect to be in New York for a short week and then to Europe to France~~
~~and won't be back until ~~next~~ November so I won't be seeing you.~~

Otherwise, the only other thing which has occured to me is a good wind
which I imagine can be arranged or more extreme kinds of pressure such
as a fence or cage confining all or most of the dancers .

Bryne

*Here is an old letter
which I wrote before*

156 9-70
*Merce Cunning ham
project*

previous pages, left: <u>Tread</u>, 1970   Photos: James Klosty
inset: Bruce Nauman   Untitled study for <u>Tread</u>   1968   ink on paper   Courtesy the artist
right: <u>Travelogue</u>, 1977   Merce Cunningham Dance Company in performance, with Robert Rauschenberg's <u>Tantric Geography</u> set   Photo: Charles Atlas

this page, left: Jasper Johns   <u>Usuyuki</u>   1981   Drawing for poster announcing Merce Cunningham's artist residency at Walker Art Center, Minneapolis
ink, watercolor, and lithograph on plastic   Collection Robert and Jane Meyerhoff, Phoenix, Maryland
right: Images from Nam June Paik and Shigeko Kubota's video <u>Merce by Merce by Paik</u>, 1978

following pages: <u>CRWDSPCR</u>, 1993   David Tudor (foreground) and Merce Cunningham Dance Company in performance   Photo: Jack Vartoogian

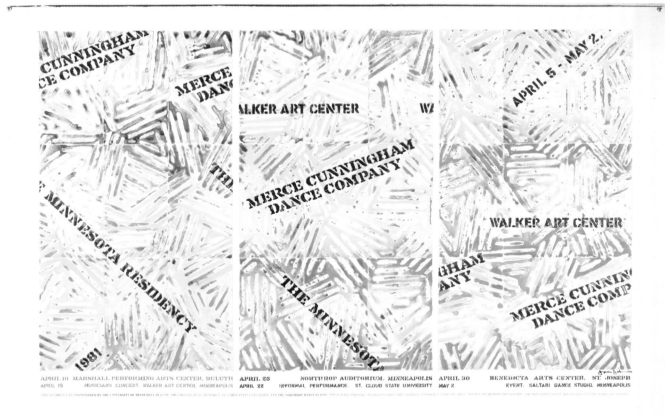

Scenario, 1997
Merce Cunningham and Company in rehearsal,
with costumes by Rei Kawakubo   Photos: Timothy Greenfield-Sanders

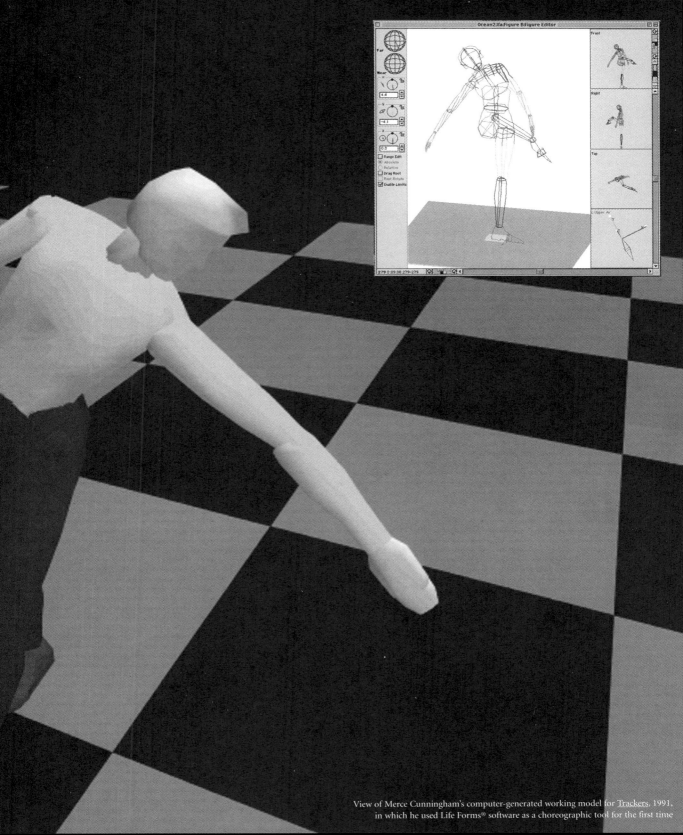

View of Merce Cunningham's computer-generated working model for <u>Trackers</u>, 1991,
in which he used Life Forms® software as a choreographic tool for the first time

Curator's Introduction

Meredith Monk in Conversation with Deborah Jowitt   68
November 15, 1997   New York

Meredith Monk in Conversation with Jamake Highwater   80
November 10, 1997   Seattle

66

Meredith Monk was once characterized by <u>The New York Times</u> as "one of America's most brilliant and unclassifiable theatrical artists," and indeed, the richly multifaceted nature of her work has caused her to be embraced and lauded by artistic communities ranging from new music and opera to theater, dance, film, and the visual arts. Monk's work is at once all of these things, but she is perhaps best described as a composer—of music, of sound, of movement, of visual images. In her thirty-some years as an artist and performer, she has created more than a hundred indelible works that position her as one of the truly interdisciplinary voices in the art of the twentieth century.

It is her voice that forms the nucleus of this richly layered practice. Unlike many composers of her generation, she has steadfastly resisted the incorporation of technology into her music, preferring instead to investigate the potential of the human instrument as something pure and limitless. She approaches the process of creating her pieces with the verve of an inventor, arriving at her nonverbal, elemental forms through a visceral exploration of the voice itself.

Within the rich ambiguity and fragmentation of much of Monk's vocal and performance work lies a meticulous structure, assembled with the care of an artisan and honed with her unique tools: a three-octave range, an innate sense of the visual and the tactile, and a core of rhythm that informs the whole of her art. Structural relationships, be they physical, cosmological, time-based, or narrative, are explored through myriad lenses ranging from the eyes of a child to the technologies of our past and future. The notion of layering central to Monk's artistic activity reveals itself in the metaphors she often chooses to express her creative approach to the work: archaeologist, mosaicist, weaver, explorer, portraitist. The landscapes she creates in her music-theater pieces telescope from overall aura to physical minutiae, with space, objects, movement, and light as carefully considered as musical notes. In each work, as in a painting, her hand is evident throughout.

The notion of imagery is for Monk one that embraces the experience of all of the senses. Her work resounds with direct auditory and visual impact, though she is equally interested in the associations and subtleties conjured through the impressions of the viewer/listener who allows imagination and memory to color and shade the experience. She has often acknowledged that her creative sensibility is one of "working between the cracks of reality," naming as kindred spirits such figures as Jean Cocteau and Buster Keaton. The rich, sometimes surreal, imagery in her pieces is as often inspired by her dreams and drawings as it is by the experience of everyday physical and spiritual life.

The sense of history and myth that echoes throughout the work is made thoroughly contemporary by Monk's deft balancing act between the serious and the humorous, the everyday and the unexpected, the literal and the abstract. She has been one of performance's most insistent explorers of character and situation, creating a remarkable array of personas that speak to notions of gender, community, time, and transformation in a manner at once intimate and universal. Broad strokes are painted through simple means. Her resolutely interdisciplinary approach is reflected in her practice of creating possibilities—not only for interpretation, but for the performative experience itself.

From the beginning of her artistic career, Monk has pushed this notion. Since 1967 she has created site-specific work, always challenging traditional notions of the performance space by presenting work in different physical sites in which scale and its augmentation can be investigated, and by working with materials unexpected in the performance arena. Since 1966, she has been a leader in the practice of integrating original film into live productions, a facet of her work that developed into her award-winning full-length films of the 1980s and still figures strongly in recent projects. In addition to her activities as a solo performer, her collaboration since 1978 with her Vocal Ensemble, a group trained in her extended vocal technique, has allowed her to expand her scope, adding still more layers of possibility to her work.

Monk has consistently been a pioneer, her numerous achievements culminating in 1995 with the prestigious MacArthur Fellowship. She continues to create pieces on both a broad and intimate scale that reflect a fusion of artistic forms and traditions as well as her own rigorous invention in the performing, visual, and media arts. The marriage of these disciplines in her work is explored on these pages, which provide discussion and documentation of an essential career that holds within its remarkable diversity a visionary creator and a magical performer.

Siri Engberg

Deborah Jowitt began to dance professionally in 1953, to show her choreography in 1962, and to write a regular dance column for The Village Voice in 1967. Jowitt was a founding member of Dance Theater Workshop and the Dance Critics Association. Her articles on dance have been published in a variety of newspapers and specialized journals. Jowitt's books include the recent monograph Meredith Monk (1997), which she edited, and her third book, Time and the Dancing Image (1988), won the de la Torre Bueno Prize in 1989. She is a teacher and choreographer at New York University's Tisch School of the Arts.

1. Part I of Vessel: an opera epic (1971) took place in Monk's New York loft, Part II in The Performing Garage (a nonproscenium theater), and Part III in a Soho parking lot. A bus was rented to transport the audience from one space to another.

Meredith Monk in Conversation with Deborah Jowitt

Following series of video stills from
Education of the Girlchild (Part II), 1973

DEBORAH JOWITT: *I want to start with a really big question. The concert music, the large music-theater pieces, the smaller pieces, the films, and the dances from the early days—to me they have a very consistent kind of vision. Certain threads seem to bind them together. Can you talk about that?*

MEREDITH MONK: A sense of multidimensionality. I think there is a way of structuring any medium with the concept of layering—layering and transparencies. And an attempt to get down to the bone, essentially.

DJ *To the bones of your subject, whatever it is.*

MM To the bones of the form, the bones of what needs to be said in whatever medium it is.

DJ *When you speak about layering and transparencies, are you speaking about seeing one layer through another?*

MM Or letting one resound from another. Or the way layering would structure how something is put together. Light or luminosity is created by the way elements are juxtaposed. In a sense, they become reflective. There is a radiance that comes from putting different things together.

DJ *When we talk of things happening at the same time, I think of Merce Cunningham. In his art, the dance and the music and the decor are separate, independently composed layers that strike against each other in curious ways.*

MM In the sense of different worlds coexisting, I was also thinking of John Cage at that moment. I remember when I did Vessel[1] in 1971, the first part took place in my loft on Great Jones Street. It was a very silent piece, but it happened that there was a rock-and-roll band that rehearsed in a studio down the street. They were playing really loudly during the performance and it disturbed me that my silence was being violated. I thought that the band's music would destroy the concentrated, mysterious ambience of the piece. Then I thought of John and how funny that notion would be to him. A sense of transparency allows for one to do a piece that could exist with anything else happening at the same time; it would not destroy the integrity of it.

DJ *One of the interesting things about the part in the parking lot was trying to decide what belonged to it—which was actually pretty clear—and what didn't.*

MM I liked working with the audience's perception of the piece expanding and expanding, until one wasn't sure how far it could go. When the church across the street lit up and the three people with gray hair waved, you realized that the edges of the parking lot were not the boundaries of the piece. I actually tried to rent a helicopter so that the sky was also part of it.

In the loft part, there was a telephone in the room that was my regular telephone. Ping Chong, playing the host, was the guide or emcee of the piece. I gave him directions that if someone happened to call he should answer it and just say, "Meredith is in a performance," or "A performance is happening at this moment." Pablo Vela (my longtime colleague and assistant director) told me that he was in the audience when a call actually happened and at that moment his whole idea of theater totally exploded. Were we really in a performance, or were we really in my house and this was a real telephone call? Everything just started turning upside down for him. I like to allow for that.

DJ *It's like that wonderful moment in* Break *(1964), which was one of your first early dance solos. When you left the stage and ran up the aisle and stood among the audience looking back at the stage—that had that same kind of shock for me.*

MM I was thinking of empty space. How would you get the feeling that we were all looking at the absence of figure. I guess I could have gone offstage, which would have been another solution. But I liked the idea that the performer was looking back at the empty space as well.

DJ *Going offstage would have been utterly different. Because all of a sudden you weren't bound by that proscenium. You were outside with us.*

MM That is why prosceniums rarely interest me. I do everything in my power to break down that situation.

DJ *I thought that those early spectacles of yours, like* Juice *(1969)[2] and* Vessel, *were really all about breaking open a proscenium space.*

MM Or the situation of audience/performer. I was really investigating the performer/audience relationship and trying to work with variations in terms of scale and proximity. The irony of some of the things I was doing—like Juice or some of the Tour Series (1969–1971)—was that the audience was mobile and the performers were immobile. The audience walked by still figures in different parts of the building. In a way, you can fulfill some of these ideas with a camera a lot easier than you can in performance. You can zoom in, you can do close-ups, you can do fast cuts of disjunctions of space and time. Different kinds of audience/performer relationships have always interested me in one way or another.

2. Juice: a theatre cantata in 3 installments began at the Solomon R. Guggenheim Museum in New York. A month later, the second part was presented at Barnard College's Minor Latham Playhouse, and one week later, the third installment—an installation with video and all the objects from the first two parts—was exhibited at The House Loft in New York.

3. In the first installment of <u>Juice</u>, spectators sat in the lobby of the Guggenheim and looked up at performers on the ramps, then walked up the ramps to view various performed modules, then looked over the edges to see the performers gathered in the lobby below.

I was also trying to break down habitual ways of thinking about the act of going to performance. I made pieces to be performed at different times of day or pieces that took place over a period of time in different locations, incorporating memory as part of the experience.

DJ *At one time you said <u>Juice</u> was about architecture; the content was architecture because the first part took place in the Guggenheim Museum. It seems to me that one of the things your pieces in nontraditional spaces do is make the audience see that space—really see it. I had never been as aware of the ramps of the Guggenheim as when I had to hunt for the dancers in <u>Juice</u>. Or when I saw them from the bottom, ranged along the spiraling ramp.[3]*

MM And the building spinning. Do you remember when we were running against the spiral so that the building seemed to spin? I was thinking about architecture as structure at that time. <u>Juice</u> became a dialogue about how space affects images and time. I still like to work with a counterpoint of my ideas and images, and a particular space—to excavate a space and let it speak.

DJ *I think some of the early 1960s Happenings artists had an idea that taking their work into new spaces would sort of democratize the art. The figures would blend with the ground, so to speak. There would be less of the traditional art-viewing situation. But they didn't often structure an event meticulously onto a space the way you did.*

MM I think that the visual artists were coming from a non-time medium. The way I think of time is as a sculptural, fluid medium. I can compress it, extend it, twist it, interrupt it. Coming from a musical background makes me very sensitive to rhythm. That is really the ground base of everything I do.

DJ *In your music-theater pieces, time becomes not just something to be manipulated, but a subject, because some of those layers that you have been talking about are also layers of time.*

MM Historical time.

DJ *When did your archaeological sensitivity to time crop up?*

MM I've always had a fascination with the notion of simultaneity. It's something that I always like about live theater, which is more difficult to achieve in film. In a strange way, film is a more linear medium. You can imply simultaneity by intercutting, but short of multiple images you don't feel it as viscerally. What I love about live performance is that the audience can choose where its focus is. You can offer it a very complex experience of simultaneity. Taking it a step further: sometimes I have the sensation that everything in history is simultaneous. It's like looking through one thing to see the next thing and that starts to inform and illuminate the next layer.

DJ *You have used that idea very literally—I hesitate to use that word—in two films, <u>Book of Days</u> (1988/1989) and <u>Ellis Island</u> (1981). In <u>Book of Days</u>, a contemporary group of workmen blow up a wall and behind that wall is a medieval town in France.*

MM When I was beginning work on the film, a film producer told me that something like that really happened. I remember seeing in Frankfurt years ago that they were also doing some digging to put a new building in and they were coming across all these artifacts. I took it a little further. What would happen if you took this wall and then behind that was the whole town, intact.

4. Dolmen Music (1979) is a piece of vocal and instrumental music that originally figured as a section of Recent Ruins.

DJ *Your heroine, the little girl in* Book of Days, *foresees the future. When the present-day workmen burst into that past town, they see her crude drawing of an airplane on the wall.*

MM I've always been interested in time travel. I like the idea of displacement—of us looking at the Middle Ages from our very specific point of view and then our world being seen through the fresh eyes of someone from the Middle Ages. So in the film, I include very contemporary ways of seeing and behaving. For example, there is a series of scenes where television newscasters interview the medieval characters. I like the idea that we are asking questions about things that really matter to us now, but the medieval characters have no idea what we are talking about. It wouldn't be in keeping for a person to ask, "Are you happy?" This idea of "happiness" is a romantic notion that is historically a recent development.

The main character, Eva, has visionary qualities. She is a character who travels psychically through time, or you could think of her as beyond time. She sees images from our time but she can't decipher them. I am intrigued by this idea of time as spirals, loops, figure eights, DNA molecule structures. Time offers very rich possibilities for weaving.

DJ *You have used that notion of time in so many different ways. In* Quarry *(1976), you created separate "zones" around the bed of a sick child, your central figure. A biblical couple occupies the same performance space at the same time as a European World War II Jewish couple. In* American Archeology #1 *(1994), inhabitants of Roosevelt Island in various eras appeared simultaneously. There was an archaeologist in* Recent Ruins *(1979).*

MM In Recent Ruins there were a bunch of archaeologists.

DJ *I felt as if the actions were like shards that the spectator had to piece together.*

MM I think Recent Ruins was an unusual investigation because in that piece I actually took the elements apart. Usually my large composite pieces are mosaics or weavings of many means of perception: music, movement, objects, and light put together into a complex whole. But when I tried to put images with Dolmen Music (1979),[4] for example, it didn't work at all. I just went right back to the music standing alone as an overture.

The next part of Recent Ruins became more like a theatrical section that included the group of archaeologists from all different periods and the main archaeologists on a platform putting a pot together from shards. On a screen behind them was a giant hand drawing contemporary objects, as if the hand belonged to an archaeologist five hundred years from now looking at our late twentieth-century objects from the point of view of the future.

The third part combined primordial, gestural movement with a cappella vocal chants. That section had a sense of irony because it conjured up an imagined, ancient society, and yet the relics or residue that it left (by people making chalk marks on the floor) were symbols like $E=mc^2$ or the infinity sign.

I thought of the last part as an image section. Image and sound. The images were bright flashes, in a totally dark room, of giant white turtles moving across the floor and huge white bees and spiders in the air—animals that existed in ancient times and have not changed or evolved over millions of years. At the same time, there was a tape of the last section of Dolmen Music playing, so it came full circle.

5. Describing the sound environment in 16 Millimeter Earrings, Monk says, "The components included a vocal phrase with the phoneme 'nota,' a text which intercut sentences from Wilhelm Reich's The Function of Orgasm with a description of a large and expansive dance, contrasting with the tiny movements that I was performing on stage and the sound of a frenzied crowd chanting."

So how <u>Recent Ruins</u> was put together was unusual for me. It wasn't like taking small tiles and placing them in a mosaic, or taking little strands and weaving them together into a larger whole. The structure itself had a more monolithic, hewn continuity. It dealt with isolating and intensifying the various elements.

DJ *You've used the term "visual rhyming" in relation to your work, especially in relation to the multimedia pieces—the pieces that use film as well.*

MM I started thinking about that when I was making <u>16 Millimeter Earrings</u> (1966), which was a very important piece for me. I saw that I could make a performance form that had a sense of poetry, nonverbal poetry—a theater of images, sounds, and textures—and by weaving various elements together, a very powerful and multidimensional experience could occur. I started seeing how you could work with images and sound in a painterly way to create or reflect another level of reality—the relativity of reality.

DJ *At that time I wasn't so sensitive to the musical element.*

MM <u>16 Millimeter Earrings</u> was very important to me because it was also the first time I composed a full score of music from beginning to end. Before that time I had done taped sound and some vocal work in my pieces, but there was a lot of silence in them.

In <u>16 Millimeter Earrings</u>, I created an additive sound environment made up of live phrases or blocks of vocal music, text, or sound, which set off tape loops of fragments from the live performance.[5] As each layer was added, the sound texture became thicker and richer. I worked on it with my cousin, Daniel Zellman, who is a sound engineer. At that time there weren't portable multitrack tape recorders, so we used four tape recorders in the performance. I was very aware of trying to create a sound environment for the images, like a visual and aural rhyme.

DJ *Speaking of visual rhyming, I was very much aware of how the flames in the films equated with the red streamers that blew up out of the trunk and the red hair.*

MM My red hair, which I had dyed especially for the piece, and a bright red wig. I was working with these different textures, like taking one image, say the image of fire, and then exploring different textural ways of working with it, which is a lot like how I was working with <u>Volcano Songs</u> (1994). A lot of people who came to see <u>Volcano Songs</u> thought I was coming back to some basic principles about my work. In a sense the images in <u>16 Millimeter Earrings</u> were emblematic, but not of anything other than themselves. I was thinking of the stage as a canvas, thinking like a painter. I worked with a sense of the tactility of surfaces and layers in a literal, physical way.

At a certain point in the piece I was wearing an off-white dress that I had made from fisherman's net. Through the dress you could see my white underwear and over the dress I put on a red-and-white bathrobe for another section. Later I put a white paper dress over that and wore a bright red wig. I was working with color and texture (the reds and whites, the net, paper, hair, metal Slinky, wooden trunk) in a very conscious way. I put a white metal cagelike dome over my head that was half covered with white screening material. A film of my face was projected onto the dome and covered my real face. The image was larger than life-size so it looked like I had a huge head. Then I

wiped my real hand across the filmed eyes. This motif of covering or layering was a basic principle of the piece.

DJ *In Volcano Songs, which came almost thirty years later, I was very aware of surfaces also, and textures. But in that piece, the images and sounds seem to be more about different characters, different aspects of characters.*

MM In 16 Millimeter Earrings I was also thinking about that, but I was determined not to do that as a performer. That seemed to be part of my idea in those days of being only a figure. The image was everything. I actually had named the character with the red wig for myself, but I didn't do much except the actions that went with that image, although I probably did more than I thought despite myself.

But I think now I have dug in even deeper as a performer because with singing you just start excavating from the inside out, so to speak. The medium etches you. With Volcano Songs, I was interested in transformation coming from the unadorned, vulnerable performer. That is something I have been working with during the last few years. The Politics of Quiet (1996) is similar in that when there is a transformation, it is not really done through costumes or objects but from within the body, from within the live person. Yet you still see a transformation coming from that person.

DJ *Whenever you've sung, even something like Songs from the Hill (1976), which is not fully produced theatrically, I feel that different characters come through your voice. In Volcano Songs it's as if we cut through layers of "this is Meredith Monk standing before me singing" to "this is a very old woman on a mountaintop" to "this is some primordial sound I can't identify." Those characters that you say come from your being come out through your voice very clearly.*

MM I become more and more aware of performance being a place of transformation. With Volcano Songs I was trying neither to pull in the attention of an audience nor to project out at it. I wanted to see if I could, in a sense, be open and vulnerable enough for the currents, energies, or personas to emerge—like abstract portraits. Again, if I were trying to delineate these "personas" in a literal way, then I would want everyone in the audience to know exactly what they were and have exactly the same reaction. But, in fact, I am trying to leave a lot of space so people can hook in, in their own way. This freedom is something interesting to me as part of the process of integrating the insights that I gain in my life with my work.

In 16 Millimeter Earrings it was very safe for me as a performer. In a way, I didn't even have to perform the piece once it was all worked out in my mind. Every element was totally controlled, carefully constructed. Alfred Hitchcock always used to say he really didn't have to shoot the film because it was all worked out in meticulous detail before he shot it. And shooting it for him was sometimes boring. While I still like to work with the same rigor, the same attention to detail that I used for 16 Millimeter Earrings, I now prefer to allow for a more immediate and risky situation for the performer. In Volcano Songs there are potential pitfalls along the way from beginning to end. It may not be apparent, but it's very touch-and-go as a performer. You have to be relaxed and yet concentrated enough to not get in the way of the material streaming through.

DJ *Did your discovery of different ways to use your voice change how you worked on your pieces?*

6. Sarah Lawrence College, Bronxville, New York, from which Monk graduated in 1964.

You said at one point that "the voice could be as flexible as the spine." It seemed to me that you began to use your voice and that sensibility more in your pieces.

MM That was a revelation I had around 1965. I had come from a musician's family, and as a teenager I was singing lieder and folk music and realizing that wasn't what I really wanted to do. I didn't want to be an interpretive artist. Even when I got to Sarah Lawrence,[6] I had glimpses of how to work with the voice and movement, combined with images. When I first came to New York I made solos and small group pieces using gestural movement, sound, and images inspired by cinematic syntax. I missed singing a lot, so I would sit at the piano and do regular classical vocalizing. One day I had a revelatory moment and realized I could work with my voice the way that I had with my body. At Sarah Lawrence, I had worked very hard to create a personal movement vocabulary and an idiosyncratic choreographic style from my own physical rhythms and impulses. That day at the piano, I saw that I could literally make a vocabulary built on my own vocal instrument and that within the voice there were limitless possibilities of timbre, texture, landscape, character, gender, ways of producing sound.

I started widening the ends of my range and experimented with my breath, my diaphragm, vocal gestures such as sighing, whispering, laughing, and various head and body resonances. I found that within one voice are male and female, all ages, shades of feeling that we don't have words for. I was lucky to have the vocal instrument given to me as part of my family legacy. I could work in a virtuosic way with those discoveries.

74

DJ *You were doing things that would make some singers say, "Oh, my God, I couldn't possibly do that."*

MM I never really thought in those terms, because it was so natural for me. Because my family members were musicians, that moment was also a way of coming home. It had such a sense of rightness that I just flew from that point on. I went back to playing keyboard. I had played piano as a child but chose the organ because of the sustained quality and possibility of epic scale that the organ implied. I didn't start playing the piano again until a few years later. I liked the lyrical richness of the piano and the ways it registered the effort of the hands. It seemed to have much more of the emotional quality that I was looking for at that time. From the beginning, I was working with what I would call "abstract song forms," which had the abstract qualities of dance or of painting, using the voice as an instrument without words.

DJ *And your body moves a little bit as you sing, and somehow shapes the voice. The choice to use no words, to use syllables, did that have to do with wishing to get closer to a kind of abstraction, to avoid the literal?*

MM Yes. Right from the beginning I sensed that the voice could speak louder and more eloquently than a particular text could; that the voice itself was a language that spoke directly and had the possibility of universality. So I felt that words just got in the way.

DJ *You can be understood, in effect, all over the world.*

MM We have been fortunate enough to travel all over the world. People respond to the music very directly, very emotionally.

DJ *Musicologists have pointed out that some of your harmonies and*

7. The House was formed during 1968–1970 and was comprised of Ping Chong, Blondell Cummings, Signa Hammer, Lanny Harrison, Dick Higgins, Mark Monstermaker, Monica Moseley, Lee Nagrin, Coco Pekelis, and Daniel Ira Sverdlik.

8. Meredith Monk and Vocal Ensemble was put together in 1978 and includes Carlos Arévalo, Theo Bleckmann, Thomas Bogdan, Janis Brenner, Allison Easter, Dina Emerson, Emily Eyre, Katie Geissinger, Ching Gonzales, Stephen Kalm, Allison Sniffin, and Randall Wong.

your intervals and your practices—things that sound like throat singing and hock-eting and overtone singing—are not as related to Western musical practice as to that of other continents and other countries. Were you influenced by any non-Western forms?

MM That has always been a misunderstanding. There are people who do learn the styles from other cultures or they study with a teacher, and they incorporate that into their music. That is a perfectly valid way of working. But I have worked very directly with my own voice and body, and when you do that and you are not just stay-ing with the Western vocal tradition, you come upon sounds within your own vocal instrument that could be termed "transcultural." For example, if I, by my own exploration, come across the glottal break—the place where the lower reg-ister becomes the upper register—that break, which is usually smoothed over in Western technique, becomes a rich area to explore. That break is used in the music of many cultures: Swiss yodeling, cowboy music, Balkan, and African music, for example. Its use and my way of using it is something that I discov-ered from my own voice, yet sometimes it can make people have a memory of these other cultures.

There are always two aspects. One is that each of our voices is totally unique, so my vocal chords are different from anyone else's. And then the other is that when you work honestly with your own instrument you become part of what I call "the world vocal family"—within one voice is the whole world.

DJ *Also the images you suggest are both very specific and somehow archetypal.*

MM For me, it's more how do I find new voices within myself? How do I not rely on my old habits? How do I discover something new in my own perception of the world? That's basically been my question for more than thirty years. It seems that even within the voice, each piece creates its own world and then I have to stay within that world. The world of that piece already exists; the music is part of that world. So that is what makes each piece unique, even though my style is very recognizable.

DJ *You've always drawn on the creativity of your performers or the personas that they can project, I mean from the early days of The House[7]—Lanny Harrison and Lee Nagrin, Coco Pekelis—they contributed a lot to your work. Now you have been working with highly trained singers. How do their individual vocal styles feed you or affect what you are writing for them?*

MM I've been privileged to work with extraordinary people over the years. I have always tried to work with and balance a group of unique individuals in every way: in looks, voices, personalities, racial and ethnic backgrounds, presences. Even in a very tight ensemble, each person has his or her own space and it's extremely clear. There is no blending or mistaking one person for another. The House consist-ed of people who came from many different disciplines: movement, visual art, music, literature, science, crafts—brilliant and unique individuals, each a world unto him or herself.

The group that I'm working with now, Meredith Monk and Vocal Ensemble,[8] is made up of remarkable and radiant singer/dancer/actors. Each is a star in his or her own right and a prodigiously skilled musician. The fact that they are all profession-al singers makes it a bit more specialized. I really need that for the music, which has become more and more intricate and challenging. In the days of <u>Quarry</u> or <u>Girlchild</u>[9] or <u>Vessel</u>, I was mostly performing the music myself. I was singing and playing solo pieces, and then every once in a while there would be something everyone sang, but it never had the complexity of the group pieces that I write now. The challenge for me with this group is to maintain the raw, rough, visceral impulses of my early work with singers who have such refined skills, while exploring new possibilities and qualities. The group is very open to trying anything.

DJ *Your working process has always fascinated me because I have never seen anybody work in music the way you do. That is, you work almost the way you probably work as a choreographer. You come in with ideas, and you may come in with something written down, but it's not complete. You work it out right in rehearsal: "Try this, sing this, what if you did this?"*

MM I like to work hands-on but I spend long periods of time (sometimes years) working on the material by myself before I go into rehearsal. I have never been able to go into a rehearsal and use material that people create from scratch. It gets me too confused. I can bring in things to play with and I can bring in ideas related to what it's going to end up being so that the performers know what I am thinking about, but it's very rare that I would use actual material improvised in rehearsal. I like to stay open to suggestions and try different possibilities, but I always have to go back to my own overview.

When I rehearse with the Ensemble, I work on the material by myself and either bring in tapes or written phrases. I try different people singing it and play with variations and different ways of voicing, so the rehearsals are very lively. In some ways, this way of working has a lot in common with a jazz ensemble, yet in jazz there is a language of chord changes and harmony that everyone speaks, but people can take a tune and improvise it in their own way. I think with us, each piece is so different that we are trying to find the language of each piece.

DJ *The way you work seems very organic.*

MM It's so much more fun than handing people a score. Because I am working so much with the "muscle memory" of the music, I eliminate one step in the memory process. When the ensemble grows with the music as it is being created, the music has an in-the-bone quality that is closer to the dancing impulse. It eliminates the intermediary process of visually memorizing from paper.

DJ *Do you think of <u>The Politics of Quiet</u> (1996) as a very different kind of piece from what you've worked on before, or a new step?*

MM It's the first piece that I haven't been in myself. I was trying to create a democratic form where everybody had the same amount of material. Everybody was a soloist and everybody was a star, yet there were very strong ensemble sections. For these performers, who are used to doing musical theater and are really great singing actors, it was very challenging to do something so abstract. I was trying to eliminate the idea of character. I was also trying to eliminate visual and theatrical tricks. I was just going for the essentialized performer—the performer unadorned, no mask of any kind. For some, it took a while to realize how challenging this was going to be.

I think of <u>The Politics of Quiet</u> as a musical-theater oratorio. I am always interested in discovering new forms between the cracks. If you start with music and put a few more theatrical elements in there, you might get cabaret. That is how <u>Turtle Dreams</u> became cabaret. In <u>The Politics of Quiet</u> the music was the continuity. I didn't want to illustrate the music; I wanted images that were a counterpoint to the music. Eventually, the piece revealed itself to be an abstract, nonverbal oratorio, or you could think of it as a ceremonial.

DJ *It's interesting to use the word "oratorio." The great oratorios of the past used sacred texts or biblical subjects, and <u>Politics</u> seems to be a very contemporary spiritual piece.*

MM I think <u>Facing North</u> (1990), <u>Volcano Songs</u>, and <u>The Politics of Quiet</u> are all pieces attempting to create a metatheatrical, metaphysical experience for the audience. I have been thinking a lot about how you make a contemporary sacred form. And what would that be? Not a form coming from a particular religious tradition, rather how to make a form that offers an alternative to the fragmented and speedy experience that we have in the world in which we live? How do we get a little rest from that? What is the function of live performance now? I like the idea of offering a respite from discursive thought for the audience, if they would allow themselves to have that. I mean, it is not an easy thing.

DJ *A respite from discursive thought.*

MM So that your mind could be rested a bit—more like a meditative experience.

DJ *I find that in a lot of your pieces, particularly the recent ones, there is an optimistic vision, or a sense that the world needs healing and can be healed. I felt it in <u>Turtle Dreams</u> (1983), I felt it in <u>ATLAS</u> (1991).[10]*

MM Well, <u>Turtle Dreams</u> was different. <u>Turtle Dreams</u> was created in the period when I was thinking about the artist as an antenna of society. The pieces were more about stating the "problem" as I saw it, even if it was presented in a very oblique manner—seeing the occurrence and reflecting those energies in the piece. In a sense, more an apocalyptic vision.

DJ *You mean as in the film[11] when the turtle crawls over the model of New York City?*

MM Life goes on.

DJ *In effect, it's saying that beyond all this speed and this energy and some of these bad vibes, there is something internal and enduring.*

MM I think that most of my work says that in some way or another. The theme of death and rebirth seems to recur from time to time. In <u>16 Millimeter Earrings</u>, coming out of the trunk after the doll is burned was like a phoenix rising, although I didn't really think of a symbol when I was making the image. I was thinking about effigy in <u>16 Millimeter Earrings</u> as well as in <u>Blueprint</u> (1968).

DJ *I remember in <u>Blueprint</u> that you finished the performance and the audience looked out the back window of the gallery and there were the two performers sitting with their backs to us, facing a new future.*

MM Those weren't us, you know. Those were dolls, life-sized dolls.

DJ *I know, but we knew they were supposed to be you. That may have been an accidentally symbolic image. But, in some of your work you seem to have chosen related themes: the artist as visionary, the quest. It was in <u>Vessel</u>. It was in <u>Book of Days</u>. It was in <u>Education of the Girlchild</u>, the traveling. It was certainly in <u>ATLAS</u>, the search for spiritual knowledge.*

10. <u>ATLAS: an opera in three parts</u> (1991)

11. <u>Turtle Dreams</u> (1983) included a film made by Robert Withers that was presented as part of the performance.

12. Education of the Girlchild was a work in two parts: Part I for six performers with Monk and five female performers; Part II was a solo in which Monk makes a "journey" from old to young woman.

MM ATLAS was the most direct expression of that idea. In Girlchild,[12] the traveling was only one aspect of a horizontal cut through the lives of the six hero/heroines—a slice of life across a certain evolution, a certain cycle of time. It's more like seeing different aspects of these characters and of the society of those six women. I always think of the solo, the second half of the piece, as vertical, because it really is one person's life abstracted and essentialized. The three different stations of this person's life are essentialized and compressed with a road or stream in between. Does that make any sense at all?

DJ *Yes, I see that too, but when I speak of quest, it was really the solo part that I was speaking of. The traveling of the group was just a motif. I thought of the solo as a journey because you started as an old woman, and as you traveled down a sheet of unbleached muslin, you became younger [see photo, opposite].*

MM I come back, actually, to the young woman that I was in the first act. In a sense, the structure is like an accordion. It opens all the way out, then it closes back down.

DJ *To me it was like a quest back through yourself to find the roots, to find the roots of what you became.*

MM That's very interesting, I never thought of it like that. Thinking back, I remember that I was excited about the idea that you could show the change of time through gesture and through sound, vocal sound. There were things that were repeated in those three stations and that is how the passage of time was implied. By actually seeing how age changed the gestures—the subtle variations of the same gesture performed by the old woman, the middle-aged woman, and the young woman—you could see the whole process of aging, but backwards. A large idea through small means. That is what I was thinking of.

DJ *Through one life you saw this. The archetypal vision comes through the very specific.*

MM It's very unusual for me but I saw that piece in my mind and that was it. The whole structure was there in one flash. I wish they all came like that! (laughter) It was just a matter of working on the material to fill it in. I also like the idea of doing a piece in which the audience already knows the whole structure; the visual gestalt is laid out right from the beginning. The piece has to unreel itself, but no other element is going to come into it. I like the spiral structure of that.

DJ *Part One of Education of the Girlchild is so full of startling, completely unpredictable images.*

MM Disjunctive events.

DJ *I remember all of the women sitting around the table, then all of a sudden they reach down and you don't know what they are going to do. And they turn around and they all have eyeglasses on, which makes, in some sense, no sense at all. It is a kind of miracle—yet so concrete and done so simply and so clearly.*

MM I have always been interested in magic, but I like to lay my cards on the table at the same time. Then, even when all of the cards are down, magic happens. I don't like to do tricks, but I still am always interested in magic, or the humor of that, or the surprise. I am excited to see and hear something I have never experienced before.

Meredith Monk at the conclusion of her solo in <u>Education of the Girlchild</u>, 1973   Photo: Peter Moore

Meredith Monk in Conversation with Jamake Highwater

JAMAKE HIGHWATER: I think we need to start out by saying that you and I are born into a world that is all predefined, and that what we really do—this is what's important here as part of your work and part of your life—is constantly redefine that world that's already been defined.

MEREDITH MONK: Exactly. Every piece is another definition.

JH And that's what's startling. The fact that you have talents in so many different media is another issue. That allows you, that makes you the Hubble Space Telescope, putting you out there where you can see what we cannot see beyond the clouds of our "reality."

MM It makes you able to be perceptually aware. In a certain way, I think the content of my work is human perception.

JH What all great art does is make us say, "Oh, I recognize that, but I've never seen it before," and yet it's somehow familiar. To me, your work is like a nation's epic mythology. It just happens to be your imagination that we share. What you've done in your life is draw together your stories, your myths, your Adam and Eve, your floods, your Noahs. And they are not the familiar Noahs and they are not the familiar floods. They may reference these things, but the body of your work is really a kind of personal mythology that is so personal it becomes impersonal—something of yours that becomes ours.

MM Many people think my work is autobiographical, but in fact I work from the belief that we have universal images, which can be read, and if you work with your own vocal instrument you come upon sounds that have existed throughout all time. I believe the more personal you are, the more universal you become. The last thing in the world I would want to be doing is a piece only about Meredith. In solo work, people often get stuck in the figure instead of just being able to read the images. I feel that, say in a piece like <u>Volcano Songs</u> (1994)—which deals with processes of nature, processes of destruction and fertility, death and renewal within one piece—it is difficult for some people to see beyond the personage of the figure because they think it's that old notion of someone out there expressing him or herself.

JH *Whereas, of course, in everything you do there is no "you" because you are simply part of the space that you're working in.*

MM Of the environment. Exactly.

JH *In <u>Volcano Songs</u> I felt you took space and changed it. It was not you who was being transformed, I thought it was <u>everything</u>. Those remarkable shadows on the floor, leaving themselves behind themselves, for example.[1]*

MM That was an idea of the residue of life or of time stopping, like Pompeii. The idea that a person's whole life could exist only as a residue, like an artifact of a person's life energy appearing in front of your eyes.

JH *For me it was a eulogy for all of my friends who've died of AIDS. It was that shadow, that memory, that mourning.*

MM And the ephemeral quality of that. With <u>Volcano Songs</u> I started working with Paul Krajniak, who's the director of the Discovery World Museum in Milwaukee, a hands-on children's science museum. I think of him as another Leonardo da Vinci–type person, artist and scientist. I said to him, "You know, I really want to do some phenomenological images, simple but mysterious." They're not really that high-tech, just a very direct but unusual use of a material that's being used by NASA now. There was this idea of juxtaposing these technological elements against the more visceral elements of the vocal work and the body— the notion of the volcano as a kind of primal force of nature against a scientific reality, and also balancing two parts of the mind or psyche.

JH *Yet the way in which you used that technique wiped out its technology entirely. You used it all up in metaphor. And that's what you always do. There's never "technique" in your work because the content and the technique are just so closely wed.*

There is another thing I want to talk about—the fact that you used nondancers in <u>The Politics of Quiet</u> (1996) and how interestingly you've been able to . . .

MM . . . work with those bodies.

JH *Yes, and change the whole notion of dance "line," for instance. When you consider what you've thrown out of the dance aesthetic, it isn't just the reality of the Western pragmatic world that you've dumped, you've also dumped most of what we once considered mandatory in art, especially in refined dance.*

MM In the case of <u>The Politics of Quiet</u>, most of the performers were primarily singers, although there were some dancers who could sing beautifully as well. I've always been interested in working with people of all shapes, sizes, and body types and the authenticity of people who move well but have not been trained. In <u>Juice</u> (1969), for example, I used four very different physical types as the four main characters: Dick Higgins, a very generous physical being; Madelyn Lloyd, a long, thin woman (over six feet tall); Daniel Ira Sverdlik, a medium-sized, loose-limbed man; and me, a short, compact woman.

As far as the dancing was concerned in <u>The Politics of Quiet</u>, in the "Folk Dance" section I was thinking a lot about mandala and what folk dance is. My first impulse was to have the weakest movers doing the simplest movement. And then I said to myself, "Wait a minute. That's not you. That's not your way. You have to let the people who don't have the movement experience have the same complexity of material." I mean a folk dance is a folk dance. Everybody is in a folk dance. This is a community. <u>The Politics of Quiet</u> is like inventing or working with a new kind of community. The piece is like a little culture, a little village.

JH *With all of the tensions and happinesses.*

MM Exactly. And so in a village, if you go to a Native American dance, there are women and men who are in their sixties and seventies dancing, and little children, and then some people are sitting by the side, but everybody is part of it.

JH *I may be dead wrong, but in your folk dance, it was just unquestionable to me that you were using the elements of tap dancing. Because of the way the stamping was being done, it reminded me of Irish clog. None of this was derivative, but I thought there was something almost humorously pop about it.*

MM I was just thinking about rhythm because I love rhythm so much. It was actually by chance that I decided to do the section without music first, so you could really hear the rhythm. I composed the music in seven-eighths time, so it's complex rhythmically. The dance is presented with only the aural stamping structure first, then again with the keyboard music added in. I do think the folk dance has a humorous quality. In a way, it's subverting the folk-dance form. It has both silly and poignant elements. By its placement after what I call the "Demon Meditation" section, in which a community deals with negative power, the folk dance cleans the space out and electrifies it.

JH *There are a lot of impersonal activities in there. In fact, when you say it's about a community, as the feeling breaks down into people . . .*

MM Into individuals, representations of the community. And from another point of view, the unique qualities of these performers. I was also working with the individual within the ensemble or within the community.

JH *Then there was the "dialogue" between people in which you have absolutely no idea what they're saying, except you know exactly what they're saying. You don't use language the way we have been taught.*

MM Rarely. I think what I'm trying to do (and it's very much the way a poet works) is put out images that have different layers and evocative potential. One of the reasons I don't use a lot of text is because text points to something particular and I want to be very nonmanipulative of an audience. So the fact that you saw the shadows in <u>Volcano Songs</u>, which reminded you about your friends that have been lost to AIDS, is exactly the idea. The images, hopefully, have enough layers of sensory and emotional compression that everybody can find their own way in there, and in a sense, come back to themselves.

JH *There's the ambiguity and the mythology, because mythology does exactly the same thing. There is no correct meaning to it.*

MM I think the thing I'm struggling with, and why it's so wonderful to have talked to you because you're able to articulate this struggle, is that

sometimes this idea of meaning becomes a real stumbling block. With my work, the language of images has a built-in booby trap of meaning. It is true that I'm not only content to present a visual experience and then that's it.

JH *I think you're more connected to the world.*

MM It's the idea of making a work that people could use in their lives, where people could, as you said earlier, go back into their lives and see something in a new way, experience something in a fresh way that maybe they had taken for granted before, or were disconnected from.

JH *Or see connections that they hadn't seen.*

MM That's more what I'm trying for.

JH *I want to talk to you about one of your most recent recordings, <u>Monk and the Abbess: The Music of Meredith Monk and Hildegard von Bingen</u> (1995). It's such an interesting collection of material. There are vocal aspects that you've experimented with that are remarkable and do have, by coincidence, certain universal . . .*

MM . . . resonances.

JH *A resonance is right, but in the new CD you show a direct connection to the very roots of Western vocal music. I don't know if that was your intention, or just because it is intended as an homage to Hildegard von Bingen.*

MM I like the fact that she was a woman who was dealing with science and was at home with healing, a person who was politically radical, and a visionary—her music was part of that. I feel very close to her in that way.

JH *The connection there was very interesting. The CD demonstrated that the kind of vocal ensemble you envision is not something just out of the air, and yet the way in which you have re-envisioned it is so totally different. What I compare it with is the dancer who just performs the dance and the dancer who <u>becomes</u> the dance. Your singers clearly <u>become</u> the music.*

MM This was something that you brought out so beautifully in your book <u>The Primal Mind</u>;[2] your notion, which is so accurate, of how Western music basically turned into a visual art. I feel I'm much more a part of the aural tradition.

JH *Let's talk a little bit about how your performers' dress adds to this sense of uniqueness because we are so accustomed to dancers who are all the same size, shape, body line, all this stuff that has gone on for years. You threw that out years ago.*

MM With <u>The Politics of Quiet</u> I was thinking of stripping down the theatrical elements. I consciously cut down on the visual elements. I wanted the audience to be able to see these unadorned human beings. The idea was to get clothing as close to each individual performer's own style of clothing as we could.

JH *I think that has gone on in your work several times and in <u>Quarry</u>, if I'm not mistaken, that was the case.*

MM <u>Quarry</u> was actually different in a number of ways. How I got to <u>Quarry</u> was unusual. I was touring in Europe at that time, the early 1970s, and I went to the Nancy Festival in Alsace-Lorraine. I was thinking a lot about this place that was taken over by Germany and France and in the process, generations were decimated. What would it be like to live in a place that had been occupied or had been rolled over by war? I became interested in World War I and read <u>The Guns of August</u>,[3] which was brilliant. Then I started thinking more about my own Jewish/Eastern European background and World War II. What would it have

2. Jamake Highwater, <u>The Primal Mind: Vision and Reality in Indian America</u> (New York: Harper and Row, 1981).

3. Barbara Tuchman, <u>The Guns of August</u> (New York: MacMillan, 1962; London: Constable, 1914).

4. Musée du Mémorial du Martyr Juif Inconnu, Paris

5. Monk has said she has always been interested in gender ambiguity. Examples of this can be found in such works as Paris (1972), during which she wore a mustache, a skirt, a man's cap, and large boots, and The Games (1983), in which Monk played the Gamemaster, a male role.

been like to be counted as a number, depersonalized, and taken away like anybody else? What was that about? Would I have survived? And all these meditations on that. How could I make a piece, an abstract, poetic documentary about World War II that had some historical references, but at the same time was free of that and dealt with cycles of war and cycles of dictatorship. How could I do that in a really honest way?

JH *That was done without a proscenium. That was an open piece.*

MM Yes, it was done originally at La Mama Annex in New York with the audience on two sides. Again, my idea was that the audience saw each other, so it was reminiscent of big public meeting houses or those German beer halls. The wall of the audience—the audience was on bleachers and you'd see across to this wall of people—became part of the whole public environment. I felt the most honest way of dealing with the theme was to do it through the eyes of a child from far away, so it was more like an American child who was sick and the sickness became metaphoric of the society, which became more and more sinister.

I made the piece as an opera in three movements. The first overall movement was "Lullaby," the second was "March," and the third was "Requiem"—all of these are what I think of as archetypal song forms. Then I wanted to create a feeling of the 1940s. One way I worked with that was by using the radio as the medium of transmission or communication, the information medium. The radio becomes a very important element of the piece, and then the radio singer becomes a kind of Mercury character, a messenger. The dictator aspect was something we all worked on. I was doing a lot of reading about World War II. When I was in Paris in 1975, I went to the Museum of the Holocaust[4] and went through all their photographs. I forced myself to deal with and face looking at this material. In the rehearsal process, I had each cast member work on dictator personas as a way of trying to understand exactly how that aspect was in all of us.

JH *Do you feel you succeeded in doing that?*

MM I feel that I have a very strong sense of my own dictatorship within. Even in <u>Volcano Songs</u> with the use of the oversized gloves, I was working with—and I don't mean this in any derogatory way—one of our ideas of masculine energy.[5] The kind of energy that has a violence, a control. The hunger for power, the murderer, the mind totally cut off from the action—all those things were within that image.

In <u>Quarry</u> I was working with something that happened in history—World War II, the Holocaust—but I kept trying to subvert a literal approach to it. I kept on trying to open it up. One way of doing that was to have a character, played by Ping Chong, who was a composite dictator. Ping's character was terrifying and he performed one of the scariest nonverbal harangues that I've ever heard and movement so totally brilliant—he was a combination of the impulse of a Hitler, a Reverend Moon, a Mussolini, the impulse of any fundamentalist kind of dictator.

JH *A scary image. You have this gift that is so unusual. It's almost a Fellini-esque gift. You're sort of Ingmar Bergman and Fellini in a kind of jello.*

MM (laughs) A soup.

JH *And it's so strange because your work is like Bergman's—very*

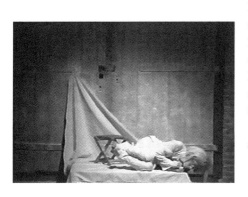

6. <u>Facing North</u> (1990) was a musical-theater piece for two performers on which Monk collaborated with Robert Een, a longtime member of her vocal ensemble.

personal, but very universal and dark at times, very, very scary. It often brings me to tears, I must tell you, and I don't even understand why the tears flow. But there's that other side of it that just knocks me out. For example, in <u>Facing North</u> (1990)[6]—which is, I think, one of the seminal works of the twentieth century— that silly dance the two of you do.

MM I don't think I would ever feel comfortable about doing a piece that didn't have humor in it. I've always loved comedy. It's just something that I feel is part of human nature. It's odd the way we're taught in this culture that there is either tragedy or comedy. Within one piece I like to work with a full palette.

<u>Vessel</u> (1971) loosely had this thread of Joan of Arc in there as a female visionary character. The piece was like a tapestry of images that sometimes had a lot of humor within them. Joan of Arc wore sneakers. Her armor was made of paper bags painted silver, shields were made of egg crates. Joan's fire was the sparks of an arc welder. <u>Vessel</u> presented a very contemporary way of working with ordinary materials, then transforming them. You saw a rake in a different way because it became a weapon, a scepter, or this, or that.

JH *That's overcoming the materiality of not only words, but objects.*

MM I like to play with that by taking ordinary things and doing something different with them. The bricollage idea.

JH *It really is transformation because what you're doing, by some remarkable technique, is making us see the commonplace in uncommon ways. Every time I see your work I think, "She can't go any further." I think, "My God, I just can't imagine where she can go from here," and yet you do.*

MM I try to start each piece from zero and that's very painful, as you can imagine. You probably experience that yourself because you're throwing yourself into the unknown every time. You're groping around in the dark and you're at the edge of the cliff every time.

JH *Another thing I want to get to is the pace of your work. I've noticed that rituals from different places have a totally different sense of time. Your work also has a variety of senses of time, but nonetheless, overall there is a deliberation about it that is almost hypnotic. I always feel this during your entrance in <u>Volcano Songs</u>, when you confront a red cloth on the floor. You walk up to it and stop, then the first gesture onto it immediately opens the whole space up. Even though I know your work as a whole predates your experience with Kabuki, in its own way it is part of something non-Western. Just as certain North African tribes also found vocal qualities that you use but that you found independently, I think you found something that just doesn't exist in the Western consciousness.*

MM Something you brought up that's very important to me is that I have always been interested in performance or music as having a sense of ritual. I don't even think of it as theater that much. I don't even think you have to applaud. It's a different sense of ritual. And indeed, with <u>Volcano Songs</u> that's exactly what I was trying to do. I thought of the red square as a place of transformation. Every time you go onto that space, sacred space, you're going into another dimension.

The thing that's so challenging about solo form is that, just by definition, it's a linear form. If I work with groups or in music I can create textures and move the focus around and I can have multifocus reality, like in <u>Dolmen Music</u> (1979), where five different vocal elements are happening simultaneously, but they're within the same tonal relationship so you can get the larger, more complex whole. With the solo form, it's much more difficult because you literally have to go from one place to the next. There's no way to avoid it. The way I was trying to work with that was to have moments of emptiness where I'm not even onstage at all. To have the projected video as another counterpoint. To have the light as a counterpoint. And then to have things slowing down so that it gives you a chance to rest before the next image comes in there. I don't think I could have made a slower pace than that, but you have to recover from one image to the next image.

JH *It was slow, but I didn't feel it was slow because I was barely keeping up with it. I kept lingering on the impact of what had already happened.*

MM But I think that for some American audiences it's slow because there's a lot of space in there. That's what I wanted. A lot of silence.

JH *It's very Asiatic in that sense insofar as immediacy is what means so much to you, perceptual immediacy and that whole Zen thing. Not that your work is Asian, I'm just making connections as an example that may help people understand.*

MM I never saw Noh drama until last year when they came to the Metropolitan Museum. Seeing those forms was so affirming for me. It has to do with shading, that subtle sense of shading—Japanese theater reminds me again of the power of focus and clarity. To me it's very inspiring and I'm happy it exists.

JH *It is the longest continuous theatrical tradition in the world. We don't know exactly how Shakespeare was originally presented, or Greek plays—we can only guess. But Japanese dance theater has been handed down through sons and adopted sons. The issue isn't that your work has anything in common with that tradition— I think it's important to understand that not only the intensity, but the beauty and the content of slowness, is part of you. You can, in realistic terms, say it's like having a flower and looking at it in detail and not just saying "Oh, it's a flower. Isn't it pretty."*

MM It gives you a chance to throw the pebble into the water and then wait long enough to be able to see the waves rather than just throw the pebble and turn around.

JH *It is exactly like that feeling. In your musical work you feel this as well. For a moment I'd like us to talk about* Facing North *and* Ellis Island *(1981).*

MM I tell the story now when people interview me about when you came backstage after a performance of Facing North and you said, "You know, the beginning of the piece is just like a Chinook myth." I remember saying to you, "I don't even know what a Chinook myth is, but the name of that section is 'Chinook.'" What I was working from was when I was in Banff and people told me about a strange wind called Chinook that could alter your mood. I wasn't in Banff when the Chinook came, but the song was my imagination of what the Chinook wind might be like. Then the section turned into something else as we worked on it. When you came and said, "Gee, this reminds me of a Chinook creation myth," I was really floored.

JH *But it's true.*

MM It wasn't because I had done research on Chinook creation myths; I had no idea about them. It was just that sort of intuitive working.

JH *Joseph Campbell would certainly agree that if we look deeply enough inside ourselves, we find everyone.*

MM That's it.

JH *At the very opening of* Facing North, *you and your fellow performer are standing in front of a model of what is going to become the environment in which you will perform. You are placing small figures (eventually yourselves) in the snowy model. We watch the process by which you, godlike, create the personae and environment in which you will perform. Talk about transformation—that opening of* Facing North *was mind-boggling. I don't know where such ideas could possibly come from. It had such a strong narrative element, yet the entire work was the manipulation of a completely abstract idea. In* Facing North, *which I just happen to love because of that combination of seriousness and humor, it's like all of the things that you are about, but in a kind of . . .*

MM . . . nutshell.

JH *. . . microcosm.*

MM Microcosm. Right.

JH *In a way you start with this microcosm, this cosmic model, and you are putting yourselves into that little world. Then the microcosm becomes bigger and bigger and bigger, until the work just absolutely goes over the edge. And it has that funny beer hall scene, or whatever you want to call it, which I think made everybody fall apart. You also had a marvelous partner in that.*

MM Robert Een, who put a lot of work into the piece, too. We had at that point been singing together almost fifteen years. Working with him on Facing North was wonderful because he had been in my ensemble for many years and we had done little duet sections but not a real duet piece. He is at such a high level as a musician, singer, and performer that we could really go to some new places. It was one of those blessed creative processes that you hope will happen a few times in your life; it's as if the piece just goes right through you and falls into place without a lot of struggle. It was hard work but everything flowed.

JH *In* Volcano Songs, *you solved the problems of the solo-voice stage work beautifully by integrating many of your talents so that you become simply part of a larger . . .*

MM . . . landscape.

JH *Yes, landscape. Whereas in* Facing North, *what I think you did was create two constantly changing beings. Sometimes you'd be him and he'd be you. Every time I saw it, of course, I saw new things. It's just a perfect example of the fact that you're not only inimitable, but you're totally unpredictable. I mean* totally, *Meredith.*

MM (laughs)

JH *Well, you are.*

MM I think that does, again, come from this idea we were talking about, of trying to come to the zero point each time. Trying to see if I can come to that level of purity, to let the next world of the new piece come through without any kind of assumptions.

That is pretty terrifying and sometimes I wonder, "Why am I doing this to myself?" It's a different way of thinking, rather than a product-oriented process. I think that in the world we live in there is some pain involved because people want to know what your product is. They would like your product to be very much the same every time so they can say, "This is what she does" and "It's always going to be like that."

I was going to say something else about the musical forms of <u>Facing North</u>. What I was trying with those forms was to make pieces that were totally interdependent. The idea of <u>Facing North</u> was two people that had been together for aeons within a landscape that was very difficult and barren, and the interdependency people have within that kind of landscape. We could have been centuries old.

JH *You could have been Adam and Eve, or Lilith and Adam, in a different kind of Eden.*

MM The musical forms—I made them so interrelated that if one of us falls down, then the whole thing falls down. I don't know if you remember the "Hocket" section, where we're throwing notes in the air. It's like being on a tightrope with no clothes on and we never know if we're going to make it through. Every time.

JH *And you did every time I saw it. Technically, I still don't know how you do it.*

MM It's a piece that is going so fast you can't think. Thought is too slow. The body actually is faster. You have to be so in the moment that if you're thinking about anything else, like "Where are we?" or "I should be getting more breath," or if you have a thought that pops into your mind—anything—you're gone. It's like musical chairs. I think it's the closest thing to meditation, a speeded-up meditation, that I've ever experienced, because meditation gives you the opportunity to be aware when a thought pops into your head, and then you try to get back to your breath.

JH *But it also has something to do with your experience as a dancer.*

MM It's very physical.

JH *You understand that thought is totally physical—thought is itself kinetic. I think that's a very important aspect in your work: the physicality of it. Not only does your work as a composer and a visual artist come through, but I always see as the matrix of what you do that you really "dance"—that it's in the body.*

MM I did come from a musical family. I'm a fourth generation singer in my family, but moving was really hard for me. I have a visual impairment, where I see two images when I look out of both eyes. I can't fuse images. I think because of that I was really quite uncoordinated as a child. My mother, knowing I had a very natural musical and rhythmic talent, sent me to Dalcroze Eurythmics as my first movement experience. It was like learning movement through music. I felt so comfortable with music that I was like a little duck in water. I was lucky, in a sense, because then music and movement became so integrated for me that I don't think of them as two separate things.

My body is not the norm of the Western dance body. It's more idiosyncratic. I think because of that I had to find a personal way of dealing with movement. When I came back to the singing, I already had the prototype of how to work with my own material because I had made my own style in my body—by necessity.

JH *The point I'm trying to make is that all the singers I know are very conscious of their torsos and their throats. But you're a singer that somehow has explored aspects of your voice kinesthetically. When I said "dance," I mean I feel that's the only way most of this has come about. It's because of the fact that you've said not "this is the sound," but "this is the body." And "this body can do these various things, and why not?"*

MM It is a very kinesthetic singing style. That's why I usually like to work with people with a combined background in which they have the singing, are very fine musicians, and have either done some physical work or are open to movement. I think the way singing is taught often is that people have to stand planted. And then if you look at the physicality, it's very painful. Even when I was auditioning singers for <u>ATLAS</u> at the Houston Grand Opera, people were saying things like, "Oh, what a beautiful sound." I was saying to myself, "Well, this person has difficulty walking, so how are you seeing that sound detached from the whole person?"

JH *And it is not the conceptual world in which you work. That's the point I'm trying to make. I think it is the song of the body, not a song produced by the throat or the song produced by the diaphragm or lungs. I think it's the fact that you have been willing to not just have the open throat and the tongue pressed to create the typical European sound. Your way of thinking of your throat and your palate and your tongue—this is dancing.*

MM It's very true. I always say it's the dancing voice that I'm working with and the singing body. It really has that kind of unity.

JH *Essentially your work is not Minimalist, it is "primal." It actually deals with all the layers of consciousness and life—those things that are not easily visible to us. Things that have been largely ignored and made invisible by our Western notion of reality. And yet you seem to be dealing with exactly these ineffable elements.*

MM I have a really hard time talking about this. I hate any kind of school or category and I have spent my whole life basically fighting the idea of categorizing at all. So I say this with big quotation marks and numerous brackets. I think the people that have been grouped together under the rubric of Minimalism—and each one a very unique, strong, and talented composer—I would say, and again I'm generalizing, that this basic idea developed from a generation of composers with conservatory backgrounds, realizing the European model at that point was really a dead-end because it was separating the mind from the body. The people trying to break that down wanted to get back to a more fundamental structure that was not a linear climax and denouement. People had different methods of dealing with it, working very instrumentally and also with patterns and over-patterns in different ways. Polyrhythms. More circular ways of working.

But where I came from was totally different. I came from the voice. I was a singer, a folk singer in high school, and my forms from the very, very beginning—from <u>Key</u>,[7] my first record—were song forms. In my mind, I was working toward a more abstract song form in which the voice could be used as an instrument. Now I've made larger forms, but it was still the idea of the song form.

When I used repetition in those days, it was much more the way that folk music uses repetition. It's like a kind of carpet that was the ground base of something from which my voice could be totally free to leap, to spin, to skip, to do anything, and this instrumental base was stable, a constant. I always think of it as a carpet. That's the only way I can describe it. It was intentionally kept simple so the voice had utter freedom to do the maximum possible. I think that's a different way of thinking about music. My idea with the voice was to try to explore every vocal possibility. Technically and emotionally the palette was always wide. I'm always dumbfounded by being put into the Minimalist category.

8. Ellis Island was Monk's seven-minute, black-and-white silent film made for screening during a performance of the musical-theater work Recent Ruins (1979). Monk codirected a twenty-eight-minute version of the film with Bob Rosen in 1981 as a separate piece.

JH *I think I can explain why certain music critics get confused about that. A lot of music critics aren't aware of what a ritual is—that ritual is myth made visual. A ritual is actually just the visualization of a myth, and without the substance behind the myth, there can't be anything but an empty "ritual." So when they see what you do, they see it as simplistic and therefore they see Minimalism, which at its worst certainly is simplistic. The [Minimalist] rhythms were very interesting at first, and essentially had almost a pop backing track. The music would become completely horizontal without any of the verticality of Wagner, Berg, Schoenberg, and Elliott. And music, like disco, had become more visceral.*

MM Like a heartbeat.

JH *But as soon as it started to be harmonic, I just felt that much of it got into grave, grave trouble. One realized, frankly, the musical limitation of the Minimalist . . .*

MM . . . form?

JH *What I thought was missing is that these composers had no voices. And what you're talking about is your "voice" in the broadest sense. There are certain redundancies and rhythmical forms—that's the consequence of the voice.*

MM Yes. That's right.

JH *With the Minimalists it was the opposite way around and the voice wasn't there when they were looking for it. They were old Baptist-hymn harmonic changes.*

MM For me the voice is the pilot. I've been noticing this more and more as I go along because some other groups that try to sing my work and think it is so simple are completely floored when they try it. It's actually very complicated, very intricate.

JH *And quite apart from its intricacy, it is idiomatic.*

MM That's what I've been experiencing. Some of the basic principles get whitewashed out or something. There are some principles you cannot convey on a score; that you have to know and have lived with for a long time.

JH *When you did the film Ellis Island (1981)[8]—I saw it twice—this is a rather personal piece.*

MM The origins are my visiting the island and being moved by the incredible courage of people following a dream no matter what. My grandparents went through Ellis Island and I had much more respect and admiration for their struggle. The film delineates the incredible pain of that experience, in an abstract way.

JH *And the decrepitude of the place.*

MM That's another aspect that's rather haunting. I actually thought of Ellis Island as a ghost story.

JH *I thought the decrepitude was part of that history; that those people lived on.*

MM Archaeology. I think of that piece as archaeology. But I was talking more about—again, done in an extremely oblique way—that notion of treating people as objects. And what that experience probably was, which was horrifying on a certain level. It's not that I'm pointing a finger or anything, but the film definitely does not idealize the situation. I was lucky when I made the film because there was a man who was working there as a park ranger, who was also an artist and poet and knew my work. He ended up taking me to some places that were definitely not on the tours, like the prison downstairs and the

mental hospital. People were hanging themselves there. It was really a horrible, horrific entrance into a new world that people had pinned their hopes on.

But the idea that I was trying to work with in <u>Ellis Island</u> was of people having a dream and enduring almost anything for this dream. When they're incarcerated there, they still find a way to work with that experience and have joy. It was really an homage to the strength and resilience of our immigrant ancestors.

JH *I think we've talked about you as a composer. And we've talked about you as a singer, although it's very silly to call you a composer and a singer because separating those two makes no sense in your case. You are a visual artist. You're a choreographer and a stage designer. But all of these things are seamless. I'm just wondering what it was like to find yourself suddenly using film.*

MM I love film because you can have fluid and quick juxtapositions of time and space. I love the reality of the environment, to put images against that. I love the dialogue with space. That's why I don't particularly like to work on a proscenium stage. I've never been that interested in sets, particularly, because I love the dialogue with a real space. I can listen to what that space is telling me. My films are most inspired by space. Even <u>Book of Days</u> (1988/1989), my feature-length film, has only shards of narrative. The medieval village in <u>Book of Days</u> is the star of the piece. And in <u>Ellis Island</u> all the images grow right from each of those rooms, the absolute dirt and earth of that place.

JH *You know <u>Ellis Island</u>—you're going to laugh—deeply reminds me of Woody Allen's film <u>Crimes and Misdemeanors</u>.*

MM I've never seen that.

JH *You might want to see it. It's a very, very disturbing film, but it deals with a kind of Jewishness that I had never seen before in which dead characters are there at a dinner table. It's a serious film. Somehow or another—your film and that film—I came away from both of them with this deep sense of sorrow and this deep sense of admiration.*

MM When I went to Ellis Island for the first time, I was so stunned by the ghostly quality of the place. There were calendars from the day the Coast Guard had left—"January 20, 1954," whatever the date was—still on the wall; the keys, the plates, the spoons from when the people were there, as if time had just stopped. I didn't go there thinking about my own grandparents, but when I was there I realized how much courage they had to go through this. They were Polish/Jewish peasants, who were put through that ordeal. Going on the boat, arriving there, stamped, poked, and everything else.

JH *And somehow survived.*

MM The idea that all these different people from all over the world came through it—I was trying to bring that out in the film. And then I became very inspired by the architecture, haunted by the ruins. The inspiration for the images seemed to occur in each room, then I also juxtaposed the different archaeological layers of the Coast Guard and the contemporary tourists, who at first don't have any sense of what really happened.

JH *There's no question that you evoke the sense of this endless succession of different people and the fact that somehow in the dust, in the pieces, in the broken stone, they're still there.*

MM That appreciation of ancestors is something that, coming from your Native-American tradition, you have built into your culture but we don't. Europe has a sense of history and Europeans certainly carry a big backpack of the past on their backs. But basically America is such a young country (in terms of the Europeans that originally came here, but not young in terms of your culture). There is still this idea of "can do." But then along with that is "let's throw last year's new thing away and plow on, no matter what gets destroyed in the process." And yet the "anything is possible" attitude is a positive aspect of the American psyche.

Now because of the Internet and the glut of information and how everything is reduced to bits of information, everything has the same value, which on one level is interesting because of its complexity. But on another level, what gets lost is the sense of adhesion, the sense of roots, the sense that you know within each moment we're living now that you and I are here at this moment, but our past is also here. Those spirits of your grandmother and my grandmother are still here at this moment. That's part of the richness of actually being in the present. It's not that I'm saying we have to hold onto all of this. You can throw away a lot, but basically there are many things in the traditions that are still valuable. That's what I was trying to also get in <u>Ellis Island</u> a little bit.

JH *I think you got into the film a sense of the thing that worries me the most—what I fear more than anything else is the mainstreaming of all the people who used to be outsiders. We go to this terrible zero point, which is a terrible point because we give ourselves away entirely. Auden said we are just distant stars flashing our feeble messages across untold reaches of space trying to reach one another. Who knows what the message is— mainly to see each other. So I think, Meredith, what you try to do, if I'm not mistaken, is you try to connect with a "world," then you try to connect us to it.*

MM I've always been interested in the mysterious and indefinable; seeing the familiar as strange; crossing boundaries of how we normally perceive the world. I like to think that I am offering an experience that could be a template of expansiveness, of limitless possibilities, of feeling more alive.

Meredith Monk in <u>Volcano Songs</u>, 1994   Photo: Dona Ann McAdams

previous page, Meredith Monk in performance, clockwise from left:
Duet with Cat's Scream and Locomotive, 1966   Photo: Charlotte Victoria

The Beach, 1965   Photo: Terry Schutte

Break, 1964   Photo: Charlotte Victoria

this page, clockwise from top left:
Blackboard, 1965   Photo: Charlotte Victoria

Portable, 1966   Meredith Monk (left) and Phoebe Neville (far right)
in performance   Photo: Terry Schutte

Meredith Monk, 1971   Photo: Jack Mitchell

following pages:
16 Millimeter Earrings, 1966   Images from a documentary film
of the same name by Robert Withers, 1980

<u>Juice: a theatre cantata in three installments</u>, 1969 left to right: Part I at Solomon R. Guggenheim Museum, New York, (detail); Part II at Minor Latham Playhouse, Barnard College, New York;

<u>Needle-Brain Lloyd and the Systems Kid: a live movie</u>, 1970 View of performance in three of four sites at Connecticut College in New London, Connecticut Photos: Peter Moore

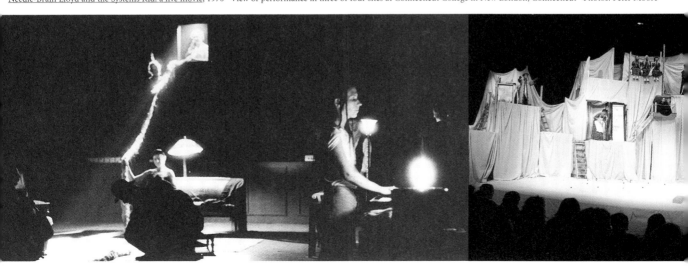

<u>Vessel: an opera epic (Berlin version)</u>, 1980 left: Monk (at right) and company in Part I at S.O. 36; center: Part II at Schaubühne am Lehniner Platz Photos: Ruth Walz

Part III at The House Loft, New York   Photos: Peter Moore

right: <u>Vessel: an opera epic</u>, 1971 Part III at Wooster Parking Lot, New York   Photo: Peter Moore

Education of the Girlchild, 1973
Meredith Monk and members of The House in performance, left to right: Coco Pekelis, Blondell Cummings, Lee Nagrin, Meredith Monk, Lanny Harrison, and Monica Moseley Photo: Peter Moore

top: <u>Paris</u>, 1972
Ping Chong (left) and Meredith Monk in performance
Photo: Doug Winter

bottom: <u>Our Lady of Late</u>, 1973
Meredith Monk   Photo: Gaetano Besana

right: <u>Quarry: an opera</u>, 1976
Photos, clockwise from top: Peter Moore; film still courtesy The House
Foundation for the Arts, Inc.; Nathaniel Tileston; Ken Duncan

following pages
left, clockwise from top:
<u>Recent Ruins</u>, 1983
Two views of Meredith Monk and Vocal Ensemble in performance
Photos, left: Pietro Privitera; right: Nathaniel Tileston

<u>Specimen Days: a civil war opera</u>, 1981
Two views of Meredith Monk and Vocal Ensemble in performance
Photos: Jack Vartoogian

right: <u>Turtle Dreams</u>, 1983
Three views of performance, with Gale Turner (top and lower left)
Photos, clockwise from top: Lois Greenfield; Donna Gray; Peter Moore

Book of Days, 1988/1989   Meredith Monk on the film set   Photo: Jerry Pantzer

<u>Book of Days</u>, 1988/1989   top: Cast in performance; bottom: Meredith Monk (left) and Toby Newman   Photos: Jerry Pantzer

Photo: David Fields

ATLAS: an opera in three parts, 1991
inset: Yoshio Yabara   Storyboard for ATLAS   1991   watercolor on paper
Courtesy The House Foundation for the Arts, Inc.

Photos: lower left: David Fields; this page, top, left to right: David Fields; Walker Art Center; Jim Caldwell;
center, top and middle: Larry Watson; bottom: Jim Caldwell

Volcano Songs, 1994 Meredith Monk Photo: Dona Ann McAdams

above: <u>American Archeology #1</u>, 1994 Meredith Monk and cast in performance on Roosevelt Island Photo: Elijah Cobb

below: <u>The Politics of Quiet: a music theater oratorio</u>, 1996   Photos, left: Eric Franceschi; right: Virgile Bertrand

Curator's Introduction

🡢 Bill T. Jones in Conversation with Ann Daly   118
January 5, 1998 New York

🡢 Bill T. Jones in Conversation with Thelma Golden   126
October 27, 1997 New York

In a recent article, Bill T. Jones considered classical ballet's adoration of the sylph as the veneration of a delicate body type that is excruciating for a dancer to achieve precisely because it is otherworldly. His own vision, on the other hand, was one of a more "earthy, casual, and familiar art," one in which dance "acts as a microcosm of society" filled with all sorts of peoples who inhabit all kinds of bodies. Those with a strong grasp of his own choreography were "sometimes ample in body, with large spirits, lively imaginations, who brought great verve and meaning to the stage."[1] In this description of the body in dance, Bill T. Jones subtly lays out the ever-shifting foundation of his own practice: the pull between purity and honesty, the collision of form and context.

In the beginning there was gesture, technique, the impact of contact improvisation, leveraged bodies, thrusting, moving, balancing in counterweight. Any body could move with (against?) any body. And so it was that a tall "athletic" black person and a short "muscular" white one came together: Bill T. Jones and Arnie Zane. They formed a partnership, creating a style based on spare constructivist moves, distillations of the lessons of modernism as it flowed through Martha Graham, Merce Cunningham, Yvonne Rainer, and on to Bill and Arnie. But also in the contact of their improvisation, they brought same-sex partnering to dance, they kissed, hugged, held, supported, propelled, and pushed each other away.

And in the beginning there was also verse and narrative. Bill and Arnie dancing to their own everyday dialogues and personal poetry, then to the admonitions of Jenny Holzer's <u>Truisms</u> (1977–1979), and later Bill alone creating movement to the words of Toni Morrison, Dylan Thomas, Kurt Schwitters' <u>Ursonate</u> (1932), and the prayers of his own mother. The text also brought with it its context, the testimony, the history of those making the dance. Or as Bill has brought out over

2. Eric K. Washington, "Sculpture in Flight, a conversation with Bill T. Jones," Transition 62 (1993), pp. 190, 191.

3. Bill T. Jones, p. A19.

and over again, the "we" in who we are. Who's talking? Whose truth?

In 1982 the Bill T. Jones/Arnie Zane Dance Company was born. What had started as a dialogue between two people blossomed into a collective built on a shared vocabulary of choreographic form. And yes, it was made with all sorts of peoples inhabiting all kinds of bodies, and filled with language and theatricality, grace and visualization. Even in the early duet, <u>Blauvelt Mountain</u> (1980)—with its wall of one hundred fifty-seven cinder blocks—visual icons had been there. Visual art offered itself as both a primer and a system, the organization of creative language (Arnie was a scholar of art history and a photographer). Then Robert Longo came and brought some meditations on architecture and physicality, Gretchen Bender added a steel edifice and kinetic video, and Keith Haring brought his own flamboyant painting to the set but also inscribed it on the body itself.

However, in the midst of all this exuberance and energy, growing visibility and success, touring the world, developing a discourse in dance that cast an eye toward the past but hungrily consumed the future, the guardians of modernism told them (again and again), that this type of drama, this type of production, was unacceptable. The "social" was not allowed, neither was the "political"—only purity, only form, no context to implicate "us." Iconoclasm may be the hallmark of modernism, but it's not done in that way. Let us show you.

And then, after seventeen years of moving together (sometimes in unison), the body of the short muscular half of their foundation, Arnie Zane, succumbed to AIDS. Bill himself was diagnosed as HIV-positive. In 1988, Arnie's fleshy frame had fled, but not his spirit. Infused by their collective animation, ignited by a choreographic vernacular that Bill and Arnie together had developed, Bill continued making works that would stun our sensibilities, creating gestures that would move our souls.

Refusing to be fettered by what he has called "the silver mask of modernism," Bill T. Jones has encouraged us to see and to understand, to look at undulating hips and see the traditions of popular movement and/or those of the African diaspora, not "inappropriate" form. To honor the truth of race, of sexuality, of loss, of history, of spirituality, of human endurance.

In a 1993 interview Bill T. Jones was asked how he, the child of farmworkers—whose labor and lack of formal education rang out with the vestiges of the African American's enforced servitude—became an "artist," a practitioner of concert dance, a resident choreographer of the Lyon Opera Ballet in France, a MacArthur Foundation "genius." "It seems paradoxical to say that my life, with all of its conflicts, prepared me more than anything for the world of art," he replied. Shuttling between the idioms and values of the rural black south and the white world of upstate New York, where he was raised and educated, gave him the skill of being able to speak in multiple, metaphoric languages. "I always assumed that the world was a place of struggle that had to be negotiated."[2]

In human perseverance, there is faith, the willingness to meet and overcome obstacles, whatever their guise. The strong, robust, and impeccable body of the dancer comfortably speaks of the ideal, the transcendent. Yet it can also be possessed by the spirit of our pain, shortcomings, and mortality. In mirroring through form the questions and the possibilities of our society, the choreography of Bill T. Jones can "transport us to exquisite realms, but also give us back to ourselves."[3]

Kellie Jones

Ann Daly is Associate Professor of Dance History/Criticism at The University of Texas at Austin. She has written on dance and culture for publications including: American Studies, Ballet International, Dance Research Journal, Dance Theater Journal, High Performance, The New York Times, Village Voice, and Women and Performance. Her book, Done into Dance: Isadora Duncan in America (1995), was awarded the 1996 Congress on Research in Dance Award for Outstanding Publication.

Bill T. Jones in Conversation with Ann Daly

Following series of video stills from
Long Distance, 1982

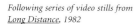

ANN DALY: You've always been a great interview. This bothers you?

BILL T. JONES: I have the uncomfortable sense that speaking about my work could historically overshadow the work itself. I look at a hero of mine, Merce Cunningham, and I wonder, having read almost everything that I can of his, if I did not know the work as well as I do know it, would I be interested in the man speaking and would he hold my interest on the page? I doubt it. I think in some ways that is what he has been trying to say to us all these years about the primacy and importance of dance as an art form. It doesn't need any exterior explanation. I think he's very proud and protective of the idea that dance is a domain, a country unto itself. It does not need literary references, art-historical references, philosophy. In fact, it can be subjected to all of those categories, but dance itself is something primary and pure.

And the word "pure" has been a concern of mine ever since I knew there was such a thing as "purity" in art. I think of pure as a child. Pure was when you rinsed the clothes until the water ran clear, or pure. Or the sheets that my mother pulled out of the washer that were white, white, white, meaning that they were clean, they were pure. That one's heart was pure and that God knew what hid in the recesses of it.

Then I became acquainted with art, and they were suddenly talking about abstraction as the pursuit of a pure aesthetic. Pure form, pure sound, pure beauty.

AD Pure movement.

BTJ Pure movement. This question of purity, I think, is in opposition to another question that I have been dealing with my whole life. That is the question of honesty and truth, I suppose. And here is where I always find myself falling into a pattern in an interview, wherein I suddenly say, how can I—a person who was a child of slaves, a person who was abducted, brought here, force-fed religion, culture, values, denied education, denied my "true heritage" as an African person—how can I ever expect to take part in this quest for purity, because the question arises: whose definition of purity? There we have taken what was basically an aesthetic discussion into the realm of politics and the kind of emotionalism that follows. This has been the dance that I have been dancing a great deal of my creative life.

Arnie Zane and I would make our formalist duets that were really about movement, signs, and gestures that had a musical and sculpturally constructivist slant. We would always find ourselves interjecting words, a little dialogue. The words could have been Dada words, completely opaque. And I guess opaque becomes transparent. I would choose words that were loaded with political, social, sexual, emotional connotations, and he and I would have it out in performance.

AD *At that point, were you considering the interjection of text as a sullying of this "purity" of movement?*

BTJ I guess I introduced the metaphor of dirty and clean, so "sully" is a fair term. But I thought what I was doing was making it real, bringing it into a more challenging arena, which was the arena that I thought united us outside of the aesthetic. That is, cultural and historical problems that we were having as a nation, as a country, as a people.

AD *So you mean "we" in the largest sense, not just you and me.*

BTJ That is very important, because there was a lot of criticism at that time of a lot of performance work that I was doing and that others were doing that was confessional. It was called self-indulgent. But I felt that the more personal it was, the more it invited a larger discourse. Suddenly the audience couldn't feign consensus. We couldn't feign anonymity. We responded. We had to respond to the fact that I was a black man who used the word "nigger" in the context of a work that had been a moment ago—we thought—purely about form, time, repetition, maybe the personalities of the dancers, but even that was not really prized at that time. So, I thought that the formalist palette was being expanded.

AD *So, you didn't see it as a "sullying" of pure movement.*

BTJ I thought it was the other question, the search for truth. Also, too, I realized that there was an ambiguity in the search for truth. My truth was not everyone's truth, witnessed by the way I looked, the way they looked, the way Arnie looked. I thought that the truth was in the ambiguity. Therefore, pile on more and more logs, more and more contradictions, more and more painful references that are unresolved and cannot be resolved in dance.

When Arnie and I were working, he never wanted autobiographical materials in his work. He had a very clear idea of what he wanted his art to be. I think he was striving for rough elegance. He was looking for the rebellious that could be cloaked in seductive form. I think that is what he wanted in his photographs and in the way he and I cavorted onstage. He knew he was dancing with a big black man.

1. Arnie Zane, born in 1948, was the second son of immigrants: an Italian Catholic from Brazil and an orthodox Jew from Lithuania. He was raised in Queens, New York.

2. Monkey Run Road (1979) was named after Monkey Run, a juke joint near Jones' childhood home in upstate New York. The duet was modeled after Richard Bull's Making and Doing, in which dancers performed ordinary, everyday movements repetitively until they evolved into pure form.

3. Contact improvisation is a partnering technique developed by dancer Steve Paxton, which involves moments of countering and opposing touches. Jones and Zane learned the technique from Lois Welk at Binghamton in 1973, thus beginning their dance partnership. They later formed the American Dance Asylum with Welk.

He knew he was a short, "funny-looking," Jewish-Italian man.[1] He was convinced that form could make everything seductive and elegant and elevated. And I went with him. I believed it, too.

At that time the whole Paris of the 1920s—Stein and Picasso and Matisse and Cocteau—they were our heroes. We wanted that sophistication and yet that boldness and rebellion that those artists represented. We wanted to do bold things that talked about form but also talked about sex and love and death. I went with Arnie, but I would insist on the interjection of a word game or a story. It was me trying to make some sort of bridge between those two questions: what is formal purity, and how does that fit into what I understood to be the truth as I had been taught it, being who I was, born who I was, looking as I looked, feeling how I felt. How could I make them fit together? Let's face it, most of the artists we admired were white Europeans. Or an American aristocratic Jewish woman. And we didn't see a conflict in that. I just thought they had laid down the ground rules—you can do anything you like, you can be anything you like, but you must do it well, and you must develop a style to do it.

AD *Can you discuss how you worked out these dueling concerns, with form on the one hand and with "truth" on the other hand, in the choreography?*

BTJ The best example was the trilogy, which was <u>Monkey Run Road</u> (1979),[2] <u>Blauvelt Mountain</u> (1980), and <u>Valley Cottage</u> (1981). Those were intensely formalistic works in terms of the way the space was delineated and the way material was introduced and manipulated. The overall impression was of watching a puzzle being worked out. And yet it was studded with evocative, provocative gestures. Some things suggested coupling, some things suggested forbidden, homoerotic touching. But just <u>suggested</u> those things, because a gesture could be easily slanted one way or another, and we played with that a great deal. And, of course, there were the texts, which would be sotto voce, or word games. Sometimes they were dialogues we had written that were cryptic but that, when you listened to them in performance, seemed to be talking directly about the two men onstage, and the two men onstage reflected an even larger set of concerns.

In Arnie's and my duet from <u>Secret Pastures</u> (1984), we were still thinking about contact improvisation.[3] A lot of the movement was grounded, with the notion of leverage, counter-pull, flux, and flow in space. However, there was a theatrical image that we were trying to develop as we were doing this formal exercise. I was a large, lumpen golem, if you will, and he a small, darting man, the professor, with a shock of white hair, who was trying to bring to life, or teach, me. So it was expressionistic. It was very theatrical, but it was not really pantomime. It was really about the values in my big body and his body trying to make something that was well-crafted, clever, and winning.

AD *<u>Secret Pastures</u> was quite a landmark, because it took on narrative on such a large scale, and so conspicuously. And in such a postmodern way. The narrative was just a pretext for the dancing. I remember a post-performance talk that you and Arnie did at BAM. You said that, for you, the dance held larger implications about the Third World and racial politics. And Arnie waved away that comment. You added that, of course, you hadn't mentioned this to Arnie as the work was being made. Right there was a wonderful enactment of that tension*

4. Last Supper at Uncle Tom's Cabin/The Promised Land (1990) is a highly theatrical piece comprised of four distinct parts: "The Cabin," "Eliza on the Ice," "The Supper," and "The Promised Land." The work was defined by Huck Snyder's childlike, colorful sets; score by saxophonist Julius Hemphill; and influences ranging from Harriet Beecher Stowe's 19th-century antislavery novel, Leonardo da Vinci's masterpiece The Last Supper, Sojourner Truth's "Ain't I a Woman," and Leroi Jones' Dutchman.

between Arnie's structuralist sensibility and your insistence that the work had metaphorical resonances in the realm of the political.

BTJ Exactly. The question might be, "Why Bill, do you think that it is important to bring the metaphorically political into the art world?" And that is what we are talking about, the fact that I thought that was somehow or another more true. It would add a level of relevance. That is a strange word to use, "relevance." And maybe only relevant to me. Maybe I truly did believe that there were certain things that I had to continue to pursue in everything I did. Now, is that what it means, "up from slavery"? I go back always to these basic tenets. Who is talking? This is a child of people who were potato pickers who wept at the Civil Rights Act of 1964, because they knew what it meant. They knew what had been denied them before. I never had a clean slate where I could feel that I owned anything, so everything had to be fought for. Therefore, everything you made somehow had to bear witness to the struggle. Now, not to say that I was at all a polemicist . . .

AD *The personal was the political. On a very basic level that is what you were feeling and doing and knowing.*

BTJ Right, which I think is true. At that time I had a great deal of pain and some ire at the sanctimoniousness of people in this world who would say, "Oh, you have management? Oh, you have sold out, you have management." Or, "Haircuts, they all have haircuts by a designer?" Unfortunately, his name was not in the program, so there was an insert. As people opened the program, the insert fell out, and "Oh, hair design by Marcel Fieve, Oh, who do these guys think they are? This piece is just a fashion show. Willi Smith, what-have-you." We truly felt that you could speak of the highest aesthetic values and you could do it with fun. You could do it with color, you could do it with character, you could do it with decoration and makeup. We didn't have to deny ourselves. By doing Secret Pastures, we ran the risk of being considered not serious, of being dismissed as glib and facile. But the freedom, the color, the light that was at stake was worth the risk. That's what we set out to do.

AD Secret Pastures *transgressed the rules of the avant-garde.*

BTJ Right, exactly.

AD *It risked the taboo against narrative, a very serious taboo at the time.*

BTJ It seems so silly now, narrative as a taboo. Secret Pastures was placing a gloss on the taboo. We were trying to wink at the avant-garde.

AD *In a very sly way. And it prefigured the intellectual, theoretical context that surrounds art now, identity politics.*

BTJ Right. That duet from Secret Pastures. Think of what we were doing there: the big dumb black savage at the hands of the small mercurial white professor, who the savage ends up killing in the end.

AD *You've talked about the trilogy and about* Secret Pastures *as two key works in which you dealt with this tension between formalist and personal concerns. Would you point to* Still/Here *(1994) as a third one?*

BTJ Or Last Supper at Uncle Tom's Cabin/The Promised Land (1990).[4] All those are big works, and I feel remiss here in not thinking about smaller works like Freedom of Information (1984), which was our version of an endurance dance.
When I looked at us doing those leaps and that unison work, with lots and lots of repetition,

5. See Bill T. Jones, <u>Last Night on Earth</u> (New York: Pantheon Books, 1995), pp. 38–39.

and I looked at Amy Pivar and Janet Lilly and Poonie Dodson and Heywood "Woody" McGriff, Jr., and Arnie Zane in his jodhpurs, I saw that we were speaking loads just by who we were together. And it was subversive, even. And our intensity and sensuality, our sexuality, and the violence that was in us—all of this stuff was coming to the fore. I thought that the tension between the formal and the emotive, or the formal and the evocative, was just there in us. Which is my belief now. The work that I am making now, <u>We Set Out Early . . . Visibility Was Poor</u> (1997), has pulled way back on polemic.

AD *Is this new dance less content-driven than <u>Uncle Tom's Cabin</u> and <u>Still/Here</u>?*

BTJ Well, let's talk about that. In <u>Uncle Tom's Cabin</u>, when my mother is praying in a very traditional way—which was taught to her by her mother and her mother's mother—and then I'm standing next to her on the opera house stage and I'm shuddering, doing isolations in the joints, the back, the shoulders, the hips, it is not <u>interpreting</u> her words at all.[5] I'm responding to the cadences, the rise and fall of her voice, her breath, the rhythm which is there. I'm trying to underline: do you see what a poet she is? Do you see what an orator she is? And this is a completely unschooled, uneducated, older black woman. By the way in which I was able to ride her rhythms, her meter, I was talking in a way about form, inside of something which is overwhelmingly expressionistic. It's worship, even. So I was trying to have it both ways, and I thought it was a growth on my part. It was at once taking a bigger risk with political statements but also more clearly delineating what is form. Or at least debating what is form.

AD *I think you're critiquing the assumption that form and content are separate. You're saying, here's a moment where they weren't separate. That you came to the point where you didn't have to make a choice between form and content anymore.*

BTJ A friend of mine, Robert Longo, used to say, "You guys aren't interested in collaboration, you're interested in collision." In this scene with my mother I'm not sure I had gotten to the point where I could say I didn't have to make a choice, but I said to hell with choice-making. That's why that piece was so big, so rambling, so jumbled, because I was forcing—just jamming—things together, and trusting, almost like action painting. We throw it together and there is a result. It will send off sparks. It will do something. That's what I was doing at that time. Was it good craftsmanship? Probably not. But was it good art-making? I think so, because it was take your materials, and then all the skill you have, and all the courage you have, and your sense of timing, and throw it in.

That's what I was doing in that whole piece, telling the story of <u>Uncle Tom's Cabin</u> in the way I did—deconstructing one episode from it, "Eliza on the Ice." The whole ramification of Uncle Tom as the black martyr Christian and his subsequent fate at the hands of the brute Simon Legree informed the whole latter half of the piece—"The Supper" and "The Promised Land." I interjected LeRoi Jones' <u>Dutchman</u> into this piece, which we think is about the coming together of races but at the most crucial point is an ugly, ugly public display of a fight between a white woman and a black man in which she ends up killing him. Already retro at that time in the early 1990s, it harked back to a time that many people would like to forget, of real anger in the sixties. Black rage was allowed then. In the nineties, black rage is not allowed anymore,

because supposedly we all have moved on past it.

AD *In your autobiography, you recall your mother praying as your first experience with theater. So there you were together onstage in* Uncle Tom's Cabin, *you making theater out of the cadences of her ritual.*

BTJ And asking the audience to put quotations around quotations. There is the tender prayer that I'm sharing with you, my family heirloom, the thing that inspired me as a five-year-old boy. There is the thing that I am experiencing at that moment with my mother. Then there is the formal thing of her speech in and of itself, and then there is my formal take on the formalism of her speech. So I was assuming that the audience was smart and that they were able to look at layers and layers and layers, of deconstruction or reconstruction. That's what the whole piece is trying to do. And you had to be quick on your feet and you had to be culturally pretty sophisticated to know, for instance, that, no, in a black church you don't dance to the preacher. We weren't doing church. This was a hybrid and, what's more, she was in a room full of many people who were disbelievers. And she was praying as if they all believed. Was there any irony in that? And what anthropological distance did they have to take on in order to be able to hear and see all these layers that I'm talking about? It was a very active thing I demanded.

AD *Your work has always acknowledged the space of the spectator.*

BTJ Yes. Somebody who wants something.

AD *How do you conceptualize the role of the spectator in your work, and what responsibility, if any, do you feel toward the spectator?*

BTJ The spectator is, number one, a person, a member of a society, and they probably come there with a need that many of us have, and that the ancient Greeks had. I as the spectator would love a transformative experience, even if I don't think I do. I would love to go into the theater and have something happen that would shed light on my predicament, being alive.

In a lot of the work that I was doing in the past, I would attempt to undercut this transcendent experience by bringing in what I took to be the nuts and bolts of modern life, something mundane and painful that maybe was divisive, when we were all trying to have a cathartic experience.

AD *Are you referring to your early solos, when you were short-circuiting the spectator's desire to be seduced?*

BTJ Well, yes. And once again, I used text to do that. Language was one way it was easy to do that, particularly when people come to dance with the idea that it is a mute and transcendent experience and I'd say, "Oh no, it isn't." Just at this moment when I have you here, this gesture is so tender, and you're loving it so much, then I will say this. Why do I do that? Why do I distance you like that? I distance you so that you and I have to work to come back together, because I believe that this is the metaphor for what all human intercourse is really about. Falling apart and fighting back together.

AD *You had to trust that your audience was willing and invested enough to fight to come back to you within the context of a dance concert, in which the attitude usually is, "If you lose me, I'm out the door."*

BTJ Yes, and sometimes I lost. But sometimes I didn't. Sometimes I was able, through the winningness of personality, maybe the interest of the movement, maybe the vulnerability that was shown, maybe some other sleight of hand, or theatrical thing, to bring people back again.

AD *So you were using the notion of transcendence and playing off it.*

BTJ And subverting it.

AD *But in more recent dances, like <u>Uncle Tom's Cabin</u> and <u>Still/Here</u>, you seem to aim for transcendence by emphasizing commonalities instead of differences.*

BTJ Well, this aesthetic struggle that goes on between the expectations of an audience and the performer who subverts them becomes the means by which the spectator can actually understand how he or she lives. This is really what it takes to live. The same process. You come into the world as a child full of hopefulness. Hopefully you have been loved, you've been taught that things are good and bad, and what have you, and then the world throws you the most vicious ambiguities. You're torn to shreds in love, and in nationalist beliefs, and in all sorts of things. But we keep going. Why? We find out that there are some enduring values: beauty, the love of a parent for a child. There is this space in our heart that I call a spiritual space that implies that I'm a part of a huge immensity which, even though it appears to be disparate and broken and torn up, is <u>one</u> thing. A thing made of such an amazing consistency that it can be good and it can be bad, it can be pain, it can be pleasure, it can be all these things. I'm saying when the work of art is good, and that experience has dragged you through it, as great art does, you're bruised but you somehow feel a rightness. I say there's something uplifting in just the struggle of having dealt with this thing. And "uplift" is a bad word these days.

AD *But when you pair "uplift" with "struggle," it seems to go beyond the cliché.*

BTJ It asks, "Do you dare live?"

125

Tseng Kwong Chi <u>Untitled</u> 1983 black-and-white photograph Collection Estate of Keith Haring, New York

Thelma Golden is Curator and Director of Branches at the Whitney Museum of American Art, New York, and the curator of its 2000 Biennial exhibition. Since 1991 she has organized many exhibitions, including Black Male: Representations of Masculinity in Contemporary American Art in 1994. Golden is currently a Visiting Professor at the School of Art at Yale University and a member of the Graduate Committee at the Center for Curatorial Studies at Bard College. She writes about contemporary art, critical issues, and curatorial practice for numerous publications and exhibition catalogues and serves on the boards of two New York City arts organizations, Creative Time, Inc. and Exit Art: The First World.

Bill T. Jones in Conversation with Thelma Golden

THELMA GOLDEN: It seems that you have always spoken in your work—I mean not just with your body and your gesture, but with your voice. You've spoken, you've talked, you've yelled, you've screamed, you've sung, you've prayed, you've chanted. Tell me a little about that.

BILL T. JONES: Well, I guess it would be easy enough to say that it is the result of an African-American impulse to testify. Words have real power and immediacy. I think as an artist I always wanted to be very direct, and I wanted to connect. This was a source of misunderstanding, I believe, for me and some of my colleagues in the progressive dance world of the late seventies and eighties. They asked what was my purpose in dancing, and I said to connect with people. That was not a popular idea in a time that was trying to understand formalism and disengagement from the audience/performer relationship. Another reading might be a young undisciplined artist who throws in everything because he hasn't learned to make choices. I think both things are probably true. When I make a work now I usually have some references, if not language, some reference to language. For me, language, I suppose, is like figuration in painting. There are some of us, some artists, some painters, who never want to be too far away from figuration. Figuration is an indicator of what they think ultimately art should be about. "The Human Experience." I am not enamored with that idea at this moment, I am trying very much to understand how to make the freest art I can make. I choose a wide range of people to dance my work, so you must understand that I am not dancing as

much as I used to. I say the dancer's ego is giving way to a choreographer's ego, and they are different animals. Both of them have their pluses and both of them have their deep hunger.

TG *At what point would you say you shifted from being a dancer to being a choreographer?*

BTJ I am doing it now. I dance much less. I usually dance cameos. I will make a solo for myself. Even in these solos I am not screaming and talking as much. Even now, I am trying to understand what my body knows about movement. What did it learn from my time with Arnie? What did it learn from Merce Cunningham, Trisha Brown, Meredith Monk? What did it learn from the theatrical dance of Broadway/popular American dance? I find one of my most interesting explorations is putting on a piece of music, like Mozart, dancing to it as if I were listening to pop music, and videotaping the results. There is a place that one goes to when improvising without the pressure of form or product that can be very revealing. Then I look at those tapes and they become a resource material for which whole ballets are built. I can see my race, my history, my education. I can see my sexuality. I can see even my beliefs about art. Martha Graham says, "Movement does not lie." I am trying to trust that. So, the speaking truly has gone deeper into my bones now. I am a very good dancer, but it is one thing to be a dancer and it is another to be able to communicate what your body knows. And that is where I am at right now. Looking for style, looking for that communication.

TG *It's interesting that you bring up improvisation because it is something I often think of in relation to your work, and in relation to other African-American artists. By way of this question I can relate a story to you. I and two African-American artists went to see Degga (1995),[1] the brilliant and stunning piece you did with Toni Morrison and Max Roach. Afterwards we were standing in front of Lincoln Center, feeling the energy of these three presences on the stage. We overheard a conversation by two obvious intellectual dance-world people who spoke very derisively of what they assumed to have been the improvisations going on on that stage. They said it as if you all had just sat there and talked to each other, and done nothing more. They saw it as the ultimate conflict between the understanding of different approaches to work. We laughed because we realized, all of us having seen a lot of modern dance, that what you do with improvisation is far more realized than what many people do with formally realized dance. Their take was that it was improvisation and we all can do that. What we know is that we all can't do that. Max Roach—what he does we all can't do.*

BTJ Right.

TG *So I guess it always comes to this issue of the natural versus the learned. As a dancer, I wonder what you think about that? When Bryant Gumble talks about his early days as a sportscaster, he always talks about how he bristled when his colleagues, other sportscasters, white men, would talk about black athletes being "natural" and the white ones being intellectual. So a quarterback was smart because he thought it out, but the black athlete who is just pure brute force . . .*

BTJ Pure intuition. I remember saying to Max once, "Do you ever rehearse?" He said, "I have been rehearsing for thirty years." I think that is a certain philosophy. You don't make a distinction truly between what you practice and what you produce.

1. Degga (1995) from the Wolof language of Senegal, meaning "to hear" or "to understand," was a collaboration with Nobel Prize–winning author Toni Morrison and legendary jazz percussionist Max Roach. Jones danced, Morrison read from her work, and Roach played onstage throughout the performance.

There is a faith and an understanding that there will always be the next gesture, and that gesture is in response to the one you just did and the one you are aware is coming. You are aware of what you just did. And through this awareness you find structure and rhythm and organization in the moment. It seems amazing that we even have to defend such a position. Everyone says, "Oh, jazz music is one of America's most truly indigenous art forms." What do they mean by that?

So I think what we were trying to do with <u>Degga</u> was demonstrate an event wherein that was the prime reason for being there. To communicate from moment to moment and to make something where there was nothing.

TG *You have chosen to use your body, to add to your body, to gesture with your body in ways that both challenge how your body can and should exist in that world but also become complicit with certain understandings of it. For example, I think the stereotypes African Americans shun about the potency of black male sexuality is something you have embraced in your work. But at the same time, as a modern dancer you have avoided the pose that allows your body only to act in a purely decorative, performative manner.*

BTJ I started to dance because I was looking for a way to express something that I felt was intense and meaningful inside of me. And this something was a historical reflection, a rumination on identity, even the identity of my family. What it meant to be a man. Yes, being a black man was a part of that but more than just identity. What it meant to be alive. When I dance, oftentimes it feels like a cathartic connection but also fact-finding. There is a wealth of emotion and impulse that is below the surface. How do I access that?

I have sexuality. I don't know if it's black male sexuality that I am being complicit in affirming. I move in a certain way. I feel good when I move. And yes, when I am moving I am sending out messages to you. Whoever you are: male, female, white, black, whoever is sitting there watching or dancing. That is what I thought dance was. That is one essential difference between dancing, painting, or making music. It exists in the body, the very place in which procreation occurs. I am dancing. I thought when it was true it would burn like a flame. And it would leap over boundaries, it would be hard to define. Sometimes viewers would say, "You were so vulnerable when you were dancing." What did they see that was vulnerable in what I did? "Oh, you looked so aggressive." I don't really know sometimes. I was not trying to project vulnerability or aggression; I was trying to access states of mind and states of feeling. The body is a vehicle through which that is done.

I think it is important to go back a bit. There is Bill T. Jones of the seventies and then there is Bill T. Jones of Bill T. Jones and Arnie Zane. A lot of these things are in the work that he and I did. They had to be. Oftentimes in the work we made in the early days, Arnie would be true to himself. He was a person who liked lists. He was not a person who liked to improvise. He liked a structure and he wanted to be able to repeat. I insisted on bringing in elements of improvisation. I insisted on being myself next to him. We in fact were trying to be honest about how we were different. And we hadn't really assigned to it racial characteristics.

2. In the early chamber duets, which were very structuralist at the core, Zane and Jones often improvised word association games during the dance, as in Blauvelt Mountain (1980): "Statue. Liberty. White. Black. President. Communist. Dog shit. Cat. Mother. Father."

3. Still/Here (1994) is a two-part work: "Still" is an internal world; "Here" is the exterior half, representing life changes as experienced in the world.

TG *It was just the nature of the relationship. At that point, just two people responding to each other.*[2]

BTJ It's strange. In the seventies, there was a period there where you could actually dance, or at least we thought we could, free of concerns about our identities. We actually thought we were joining the grand discourse around the potential of movement. We came as who we were. Our movement had been informed equally by watching West Side Story, by people dancing in front of the jukebox, by Rudolph Nureyev and Margot Fontaine, Martha Graham, and Isadora Duncan. That is what we were doing. All these things belonged to us. We were processing all we had seen. And yet there was another discourse that the critical establishment imposed upon us. We began to respond to that.

TG *Is that at the point when the company was formed?*

BTJ The company was formed in 1982, although I had been doing works with pickup companies since the mid-seventies. The company began as a dialogue between two people that we wanted to open up to a community. That was not an easy task because we had to understand the language that this community would speak. What would we speak about? We were obliged to provide for persons who were not so invested. What was the agenda?

TG *How would you say that early, initial company compares with the company that you now work with? What is the relationship between the two?*

BTJ This is one of those big questions that has all sorts of reverberations. The company in that day was much smaller. The dancers in the company were closer to us in age. Many of us had similar concerns, backgrounds in contact improvisation. We had the same kind of cultural reference points in terms of modern dance heroes, visual arts heroes, rock music, what have you. The company members now are more sophisticated as artists. They have more information earlier on, many of them have degrees and many of them are much younger. I find that they have come into an art world in which they have never had to validate their art. I came into the tail end of the fight to validate modern dance. Isadora Duncan started fighting at the turn of the century. Martha Graham was fighting in the thirties. Merce Cunningham was fighting in the fifties. For these dancers—some of whom were not born until the late seventies—modern dance simply is. They see this incredible smorgasbord of styles and concerns and they expect it as the lay of the land.

Do they know that once there was only a handful of modern-dance choreographers? These choreographers were a bit more like gurus. They had their tight little group of performers around them, and either you were with them or you were not. Everything you did was a statement of defiance and definition. I have a bit of that. They don't remember that. So there is constantly this desire on my part to shock them, maybe. To ask the question, "Where is your passion? Why do you do this?" I want them to feel how Arnie and I felt—this is going to be the great adventure of their lives. We were defined by this thing. It was not just another career choice.

TG *Let's talk a little about Still/Here (1994).[3] I can imagine that piece had a cataclysmic effect on the perceptions of the company. Certainly it entered your work into an intense public critical debate. This is perhaps the moment when your work pushed this dialogue about art and life in a way that transformed that discourse. Your work*

4. The choreography for <u>Still/Here</u> was constructed directly from the Survival Workshops for the terminally ill conducted by Jones in eleven cities. Participants "were of all ages, classes, races, sexual preferences, and states of health." Jones worked with these people to elicit personal and often very private reactions and gestures focusing on their experience. The lyrics in the "Still" section incorporate the words of the workshop participants.

5. The last section of <u>Last Supper at Uncle Tom's Cabin/The Promised Land</u> involved the communities in which the work was performed. The company and local dancers, all of whom are completely disrobed by the end, dare the audience to make a leap of faith and express an acceptable vision of communality.

has always done this, has always been focused on the art/life axis, and probably has come very naturally out of that concern. For many artists, not just dancers, this discourse allowed them to understand this notion of the validity of art and life as a conjoined concern in contemporary practice.

BTJ I was criticized because there was no distance between the "materials" of the participants and the art product, which was not true, of course.[4]

TG *You have to know that for any number of artists working with their lives, their culture, their sexuality, their gender, this is the fight they have been fighting to no avail. And to have it brought to the forefront, through your example, was vindicating for many because it allowed them now to talk about this validity.*

BTJ When I did <u>Last Supper at Uncle Tom's Cabin</u> (1990), I wanted to make a work that would talk about a lot of issues that were personal identity issues. A feeling of being conflicted. I was bred to be alienated but I refused: skeptical, yes; alienated, no. So I wanted to make this big sprawling work that talked about a "we." It was touchy-feely, because I wanted to say we are not afraid. I am reminded of a Les Levine poster in the subway during the eighties portraying Asian couples standing, sober and relaxed with a firm gaze, holding the viewer. The caption read, "We are not afraid." To create a stage full of naked people at a time when AIDS is raging, what does it mean to be naked together? Are you talking about group sex, are you talking about exploitation, what is this? Exhibitionism? Why do you want us to look at your naked body? We were not just naked, we were singing together. At that point it stopped being art and became an act of faith.[5]

With <u>Still/Here</u> I wanted to dig deeper. What was I looking for in that community? I was looking for something that we all shared. I was looking for a communality. I said, "What do you mean, Bill? Communality around what?" I looked to the personal. Concern about my own HIV status, concern about what AIDS has meant. Also wanting to redefine this phenomenon away from the idea of "the other." I wanted to understand this phenomenon as part of a continuous and cogent fabric. Therefore I decided to do scientific research. Rather than mine my emotions, to go connect with and question different persons living in contrasting situations. I would gather material and make a theater work from it. It's not an original idea, but it is what I had to do. So I thought it wouldn't be at all controversial. I thought it might be illuminating, I would learn a lot, and I thought other people might also if the work was conceived well. We would be able to come closer to these questions and own them, especially people who were not ill. That is what I was doing.

What I learned was that there were all sorts of responses that came from people unprepared for the basic issue: "How does one respond to a person sharing a painful dilemma? How does one respond when this dilemma implies an inescapable communality that implicates us all?" This strategy relates to a tradition in contemporary art that relies on confrontation and various degrees of implicating the spectator in the artist's search and questioning. I'm referring to the work of such artists as Vito Acconci, Joseph Beuys, Cindy Sherman, and Nan Goldin. What was so different about <u>Still/Here</u>? It didn't hide behind formalism. It was costumed, lit, choreographed, sung. It was a show. I thought that would be enough distance, but the truth is that one of the

6. We Set Out Early . . . Visibility Was Poor (1997) was inspired by an examination of both the universal immigrant experience and the conclusion of the twentieth century. The choice of composers—Igor Stravinsky, John Cage, and Peteris Vasks—musically spans the century and illustrates, somewhat, the changes that have occurred. The dance onstage evokes a feeling of journey and mass movement.

7. Jones, who studied film in college, and Zane often drew from avant-garde filmmakers such as Stan Brakhage and others, especially their use of repetition, speed, inversion, and manipulation.

strategies of the late twentieth century is to push the boundaries of art and life as far as you can. Mix them up. Therefore, I was rather flabbergasted by the response.

The new work that I have made is called We Set Out Early . . . Visibility Was Poor (1997).[6] It sounds like a narrative, already framed, but it is not. It is decidedly nonlinear, suggesting many stories. It is an examination of "we," a mythic "we," an epic "we." This piece signifies through movement, through dance. We are dancing with as many variations of texture, rhythm, color, and gestural nuance. There is a score that tells a chronological story of the twentieth century: Stravinsky, 1917; John Cage, late forties/early fifties.

For Last Supper at Uncle Tom's Cabin I took Martin Luther King's speech and turned it backwards. I could have taken the Gettysburg Address. Why did I choose Martin Luther King? It means something to me. But I have deconstructed it. People always do that now. Was I not ironic enough? I believe that is part of what is held against African-American artists, or maybe me—not enough irony. Maybe too much sincerity about it. And then I say okay, in our art world, a late twentieth-century art world, if you believe anything can be done as long as you do it with sufficient persuasion and confidence, then I will present sincerity.

TG *But it is misunderstood.*

BTJ Right, and then we're off. Then it gets interesting. It would be great if I could be like a Zen master and pull back, detached, and watch the discourse. I can't. I am torn because I set out not to reconfigure the notion of me and them. I wanted to talk about us. I am sharing my art with other artists and art lovers. No, I don't have to wear the silver mask of modernism. I discovered that there exist self-appointed guardians of the correct aesthetic and values.

TG *I think in many ways you are voicing what seems the movement of many artists who are working at the end of the century. That is, to claim their own specificity and take it out of this generic confine of the "we." The cultural "we."*

You have quite often collaborated with visual artists. Could you talk a bit about your interest in the visual arts, in contemporary arts and collaborations with them, and how that has affected your work?

BTJ For me, visual artists' strategies and philosophies have always acted as a sounding board or even a primer. What does it mean to develop a system? I've learned about systems from watching visual artists develop their language. I learned a great deal about dance and repetition, structure and contrast, from watching the work of late sixties/early seventies avant-garde filmmakers who were trying to escape the confines of narrative cinema. I was most taken with their use of rhythm in editing, their manipulation of human gesture, and their use of the camera in a gestural way. As a dancer-choreographer, I found these filmmakers very appealing. I tried to bring those ideas that were just acts of light in a two-dimensional world into our world—a world predicated on actual events, ordered by the body's laws and the choreographer's imagination. Trusting that flesh and bone, human beings, even if they were behaving as if in a deconstructed film, would still be telling a truth. When Arnie and I made Blauvelt Mountain (1980), we were thinking very much about non-narrative film as we had been exposed to it by Ken Jacobs, Michael Snow, Tony Conrad, and others.[7]

8. Keith Haring painted Jones' nude body for a series of photographs by Tseng Kwong Chi (see p. 125).

9. Jenny Holzer's famous works use straightforward phrases that comment on contemporary society, such as "Money creates taste," "Much was decided before you were born," "Freedom is a luxury not a necessity," or "Disgust is the appropriate response to most situations," which Jones used in the performance.

We took sequences that were maybe fifteen minutes long, broke them up, and reversed and recombined them. They became forty-five minutes long. The sequences included embraces, slaps, lifts, hugs, and whispers. What was more important: the form or the content? Painter friends like Keith Haring represented another kind of aspiration.[8] Here was a person who was exuberantly involved in the popular world. He was saying, "I dare you to come out, to come out and play. High or low art? Who says it has to be one thing or the other?" In the eighties, this was fun and glamorous. But the purpose was very serious. We were trying to make a mark that was indelible, using anything at our disposal. The only limitation was our imagination. When I worked with artist Jenny Holzer's <u>Truisms</u> in <u>Holzer Duets</u> (1985), she was an anonymous presence.[9] She stayed very far away, gave me the permission to do the work. I wanted nothing more than to engage her work and use it as I would music. Also because it wasn't traditional visual artwork, it could be manipulated for musical, theatrical, poetic effect. The words were worked into the fabric of this duet that I made with Larry Goldhuber.

TG *You have also collaborated extensively with musicians. Talk about your approach to music. In many ways the music you choose is never simply a score. It has a much more active presence. Even when you are working with composers who are not alive, you create the aura of collaboration.*

BTJ That's an interesting observation. For instance, I chose the Mendelssohn only after I could hear him, the sixteen-year-old hotshot inside of it. If he were alive today, he would be playing electric guitars and bass. Once I heard that voice, I knew that I could talk to him. I thought he really didn't want me to freeze up with what he meant intellectually. I thought, "He wants me to feel something." I am using Stravinsky now. I put on the music, and I try to dance to it. Pop music, perhaps. I videotape these improvisations and analyze what I did and teach it. It becomes a vocabulary. As it is codified, refined, edited, and taught, it is manipulated. The score remains a constant that aids in the structuring of the work. I try to choose seasoned, realized scores. If the score is successful on its own terms, I feel freer to play. It's a respectful dialogue and I trust it. I'm not interested in using music ironically. I don't use baroque music to spoof its dated conventions. I try to find what works in it now.

TG *Are there any composers, musicians, or kinds of music that you've wanted to work with but haven't found a way to put movement to?*

BTJ I had a revelation recently while trying to find orchestral music that could be danced to. Some of the best music, the music I love the most, really doesn't need dance. It's simply another medium that doesn't need anything from me. So therefore I have to find music that can be a nice partner, that allows me to approach it and dance with it. I feel a successful dance should be able to exist in silence and unadorned. Music, decor, and costume simply amplify, frame, and support.

TG *What does audience mean to you now as a dancer and a choreographer? Is it something that comes into your thoughts in making the work?*

BTJ I am proud to say we are building a pretty broad audience. I think we attract a number of people who see my persona as being about social

change. They see my company as being about inclusion, therefore we are capable of attracting some marginal persons. We are strong, generous performers, and we "put on a good show." Therefore I believe that we sometimes attract audiences that might attend Broadway. They take a chance because what we do is antic and colorful. Although I don't choreograph characters, there are characters on the stage. It's a young audience. However, I am always surprised at how certain works connect with certain people. Still/Here did that. Still/Here expanded our audience considerably. The scope of the work and the subject matter made many more people feel safe in coming to see it.

TG *I think because in some ways Still/Here transcended that narrow image of modern dance. Modern dance, like contemporary art, suffers sometimes from a restricted perception of what it can or will be. I think your work has also transformed our understanding of contemporary art. It engages a number of different approaches to ideas and issues so that we can begin to understand contemporary artists on other levels. It is not just concept versus form, but it is a collision of the two. That is where, perhaps, an audience developed in a broader fashion around these works. I think most artists today are embracing this idea that the work has to be viewed on a number of levels, rather than simply on one alone.*

BTJ I agree. This is an intense issue. I am a great fan of Merce Cunningham. I learn a great deal from him. Merce has shown me one path, one way. His path has been so clear that I have been able to see myself in a delineated, stark relief, because of our differences. It does make my way more clear. However, like any serious artist working today, I am constantly trying to educate, to be understood.

TG *Because the two are not seen as being one and the same.*

BTJ I have so many concerns, the world is so full of pitfalls and categories, and yet that somehow gets me dancing. It is my attempt to throw off all of my own presuppositions and concerns, as well as those that are being offered and imposed. That is what improvisation is like. That is what a new work is like. How can I go forth this time and be surprised? That is an attitude I believe is distinctly African American and a constant spiritual struggle. I am in pursuit of grace. I don't want to work in defiance all the time.

TG *And what place do you see yourself taking as a choreographer and a member of the community?*

BTJ Here is a man who is dealing with the unknown as it relates to this very mundane body. He believes that in it is inspiration and encouragement, for himself and those willing to watch. You are invited in. This man values sincerity and is full of human frailty. He is brave and wants you to be brave. His works are in pursuit of a profound sexuality. It can be silly but not insultingly so. His work changes, because we change. That is what I would like.

I have a friend who is a great orator/speaker. She told me recently that she has decided she has many topics but one theme, and that is, she wants to talk about whatever is human. "I am a human being"—that is her theme. And the "I" wants to be a universal "I." She is constantly trying to teach this to others. I want to talk about complexity, conflict. I want to know how we are changing. I want to know how I am changing in relationship to computer culture. I want to know the "I" that was defined by slave culture. Is it antiquated, is it obsolete? And if so, what has it changed to? I don't know if there is any truth other than the

10. Jones' only appearance in <u>Still/Here</u> is on a video monitor that Lawrence Goldhuber wheels around the stage during the "Here" section.

one that I subscribe to and can promote most persuasively. My friend disagrees. She believes there is a truth and you have to cultivate it. It has a spiritual, economic, and political agenda. I want to believe that politics is being honest, and daring to do what one is afraid to do, yet senses has to be done. Art recognizes the poetic in the political, and vice versa.

TG *Is there a way that you see the dance world changing or your work changing? That either makes you pause or gives you great pleasure?*

BTJ My work gives me pleasure and it is changing because it is getting finer. It can do more things. I take delight in making works that I want to see. I am in dialogue with great works of art that I love. And I am in dialogue, somehow, trying to stand up to those voices, those detractors who say what dance should and shouldn't be.

Arnie and I used to joke that somewhere there is a big machine that is pumping out young dancers. Every year they march into the city, wanting to be used, underpaid, and seen. There will always be a new wave. I am trying to understand dignity as an artist. I want a middle-class life. I want my dancers to have a middle-class life. I want them not to feel like oddities that are to be gawked at and discounted. I want them to know that what they do is meaningful, even sacred. I know this is a problematic word. However, it helps me to balance my "account." Let's say I don't make enough money for the amount of work I do. I think there is another kind of lucre at stake here, and that is what I call spirituality and the sacred. That is rooted very much in a communion between a group of people.

TG *Is that what you choose to work with?*

BTJ Where else do you see it really happening?

TG *Nowhere.*

BTJ It doesn't happen very much. I once thought it happened everywhere. People don't mingle anymore. So there is a victory in keeping the group together and keeping them all shapes, colors, and sizes. The movement originates in my body. They have to learn what Bill does. But I love to see how many ways it's done.

TG *So you are dancing less and less while you are actually making more movement?*

BTJ Yes, and allowing opportunities for them to enter into it and make their contribution.

TG *It seems to me that there were two really amazing metaphors that I took from that passage in <u>Still/Here</u> when Larry is pushing around the video monitor with you on it.[10] On one hand you were very much at the center of the work, mediating it all, but no longer in it. And I think the interesting thing about that is it really makes us think about your work as such without you attached to it anymore.*

BTJ There used to be something they would ask you in the advancement program of the NEA: "What do you think about the institutionalization of your organization?" And my generation—we were anti-institution. What you're describing is in fact an entity that only exists because of many individuals all organized around some idea. Now what is the idea? Is it my creative ego or is it a vision suggested by the work I have created?

TG *I think institutionalization is at its best when you do something, and put it out there, and you are given a place to do it, so it enters our conscious-ness and we understand things a bit differently. For instance, how you have used same-sex pairing in dance to bring out eroticism and romance, particularly within an African-American context.*

BTJ When Bill and Arnie began to work and we insisted that our work be as open, free, and candid as possible, some found it "problematic" or "provocative." We were convinced that this was what it meant to be free. The world, the country, had witnessed the signing of the Civil Rights Act of 1964, had acknowledged Stonewall, and women's rights were being hotly debated. This spirit challenged us to "step on out there and do what you need to do." We wanted to have a company because we needed to expand our dialogue. There was too much pressure on the two of us. Me in that TV set started there. Arnie understood this early on. "The ideas are not tied up with my personality," he said, "or my flesh." It was harder for me to do that. That is what the company was about. But within the company we still had to have that strange sort of mismatched quality that defined and informed Bill and Arnie. We set out to avoid the "doctrinaire"— all men, all gay, all black, etc.

When I am in the TV set being pushed around by Larry, I said that was a message in a bottle, intended for a time when all of the discourse around Still/Here is forgotten, and some person will look at that image and ask a question about that moment. I rely on that moment, the truth in that moment. In each moment, I have to answer one question: Can I really dance in the world that I live in? Work is becoming less and less about issues. It is now about the biggest issue I can think of—how do we live here with dignity? All of us. I am aging. How have my attitudes, opinions, and ideas calcified? How do we live constantly as if dancing? That is what the new work is about.

TG *Has your way of working changed?*

BTJ Yes, I'm making works that are in some ways more about the vocabulary than about dancing. I know that is a terrible thing to say, that is a sacrilege, considering what I think is really successful about what I've built. It seems to be what time and my desire to make an indelible mark is telling me.

TG *Reading your memoir, Last Night on Earth (1995), one can see how autobiographical circumstance can mean something, can mean everything. The artist Glenn Ligon and I often repeat a James Baldwin anecdote to each other. Baldwin appeared on the Dick Cavett show years ago and Cavett asked Baldwin (and I paraphrase) if at some point he didn't consider his life utterly hopeless being born poor, black, and gay in America. And Baldwin replied with glee, "No, I thought I had hit the jackpot."*

BTJ I realize that. I think I am a descendent of James Baldwin. However, I have a fear. It is a fear of mythologizing an "outsider" persona. Yes, our stories are colorful, complex, and compelling. Yet we are a work in progress. What happens next?

TG *At the heart of it, you want to keep asking the questions.*

BTJ I have no choice. When I stop asking questions, the reason behind the dancing dies.

<u>Track Dance</u>, 1974   top: Bill T. Jones; bottom: Cast and community members in performance at State University of New York, Binghamton

Arnie Zane   <u>On the Hill in Johnson City</u>   1972   black-and-white photograph   Arnie Zane Archive, Gift of Bill T. Jones, UCR/California Museum of Photography,
University of California, Riverside

<u>Monkey Run Road</u>, 1979   Bill T. Jones and Arnie Zane

<u>Blauvelt Mountain</u>, 1980   Bill T. Jones and Arnie Zane   Photos, top: Chris Harris; bottom: Jim Jenkins

left: <u>Valley Cottage</u>, 1981
Bill T. Jones and Arnie Zane

right: <u>Rotary Action</u>, 1982
Bill T. Jones and Arnie Zane

Secret Pastures, 1984
Bill T. Jones and Arnie Zane   Photo: Lois Greenfield

right: Keith Haring   Garden of Radio Delights   1984   (detail)
Backdrop for Secret Pastures   acrylic on canvas
Courtesy Foundation for Dance Promotion, New York

Animal Trilogy, 1986
clockwise, from left: Bill T. Jones; Jones and company;
Jones and Arnie Zane, with set by Cletus Johnson

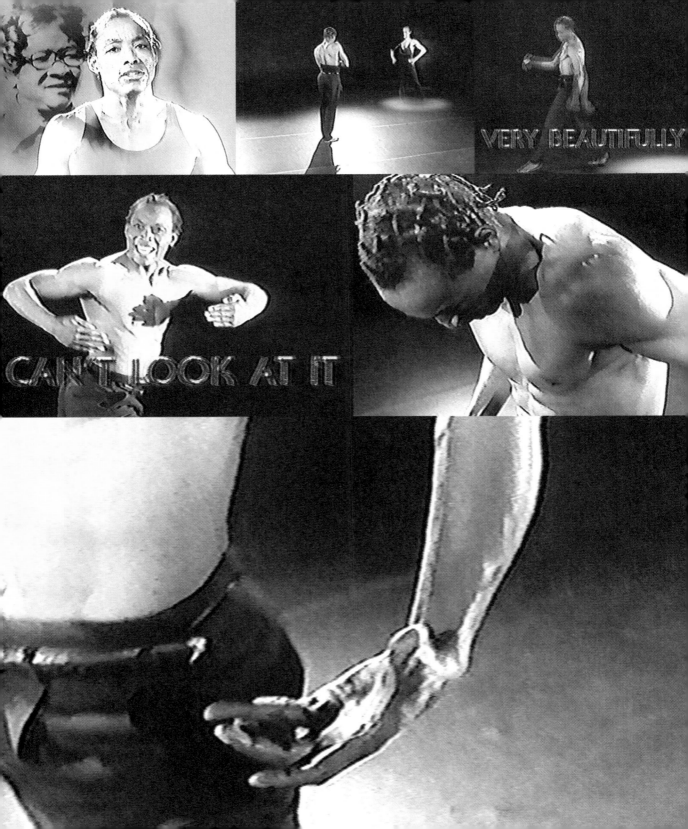

left: <u>Untitled</u>, 1989
Stills from a dance for video produced for <u>Alive From Off Center</u>

right: <u>Absence</u>, 1988
Photos: Tom Brazil

<u>Last Supper at Uncle Tom's Cabin/The Promised Land</u>, 1990
Bill T. Jones and company in performance, with set by Huck Snyder

following pages: <u>Still/Here</u>, 1993
Bill T. Jones and company in performance, with video by Gretchen Bender
Photos: David Smith

We Set Out Early . . . Visibility Was Poor, 1997
Photos: Simon R. Fulford

Abbreviations:

M Music by
Ch Choreographed by
C Costumes by
S Scenery by
MCDC Merce Cunningham Dance Company
FP First performance

Unless otherwise noted, all dances choreographed by Merce Cunningham, and all solos danced by Merce Cunningham.

The chronology presented here is excerpted with permission from David Vaughan's <u>Merce Cunningham: Fifty Years</u> (New York: Aperture Foundation, 1997).

Merce Cunningham at Black Mountain College   Photo: Hazel-Freida Larsen

Unbalanced March
Solo **M** Paul Hindemith
   FP Elks Club, Seattle

Jazz Epigram
Ch Merce Cunningham and Dorothy Herrmann **M** Ernst Toch
   FP Elks Club, Seattle

158   **1938**

1939

Skinny Structures
Part One: **Ch** Dorothy Herrmann
   M Jean Wiener
Part Two: **M** Darius Milhaud
Part Three: **Ch** Syvilla Fort **M** Felix Petyrek
Part Four: **Ch** Dorothy Herrmann, Merce Cunningham, Syvilla Fort **M** Alfredo Casella **FP** Cornish Dance Group, Cornish Theatre, Seattle

Courante, Contagion
Solo **M** Zoe Williams **FP** Mills College, Oakland, California

1941

Seeds of Brightness
Ch Jean Erdman and Merce Cunningham **M** Norman Lloyd **C** Charlotte Trowbridge **FP** Bennington College, Bennington, Vermont

Credo in Us
"A dramatic playlet for Two Characters" *
Ch Jean Erdman and Merce Cunningham **M** John Cage **C** Charlotte Trowbridge **FP** Bennington College, Bennington, Vermont *After first performance subtitle was changed to "A Suburban Idyll"*

Renaissance Testimonials
Solo in two parts, "Profession-Confession" **M** Maxwell Powers **C** Charlotte Trowbridge **FP** Bennington College, Bennington, Vermont

Ad Lib
Ch Jean Erdman and Merce Cunningham **M** Gregory Tucker **C** Charlotte Trowbridge **FP** Bennington College, Bennington, Vermont

Totem Ancestor
Solo **M** John Cage **C** Charlotte Trowbridge **FP** Studio Theatre, New York

1942

1943

In the Name of the Holocaust
Solo **M** John Cage **C** Merce Cunningham **FP** Arts Club of Chicago

Shimmera
Solo **M** John Cage **C** Merce Cunningham **FP** Arts Club of Chicago

The Wind Remains
Zarzuela in one act, after Federico García Lorca's <u>Asi que pasen cinco años</u>, adapted by Paul Bowles **M** Paul Bowles Produced and Directed by Schuyler Watts Dance Director Merce Cunningham **S** Oliver Smith **C** Kermit Love Conducted by Leonard Bernstein **FP** The Third Serenade, Museum of Modern Art, New York

Triple-Paced
Solo **M** John Cage **C** Merce Cunningham **FP** Studio Theatre, New York

Root of an Unfocus
Solo **M** John Cage **C** Merce Cunningham **FP** Studio Theatre, New York

Tossed As It Is Untroubled
Solo **M** John Cage **C** Merce Cunningham **FP** Studio Theatre, New York

The Unavailable Memory of
Solo **M** John Cage **C** Merce Cunningham **FP** Studio Theatre, New York

Spontaneous Earth
Solo **M** John Cage **C** Merce Cunningham **FP** Studio Theatre, New York

Four Walls
A dance play by Merce Cunningham, directed by Merce Cunningham and Arch Lauterer **M** John Cage **S, C** Arch Lauterer **FP** Perry-Mansfield Workshop, Steamboat Springs, Colorado

Idyllic Song
Solo **M** Erik Satie, arranged by John Cage **C** Merce Cunningham **FP** Woman's Club, Richmond, Virginia

1944

1945

Mysterious Adventure
Solo **M** John Cage **C** and object after a design by David Hare **FP** Hunter Playhouse, New York

Experiences
Solo in two parts **M** John Cage and Livingston Gearhart **C** Merce Cunningham **FP** Hunter Playhouse, New York

The Encounter
Solo **M** John Cage **C** Merce Cunningham
   FP Hunter Playhouse, New York

Invocation to Vahakn
Solo **M** Alan Hovhaness **C** Merce
   Cunningham **FP** Hunter Playhouse,
   New York

'Fast Blues'
Solo **M** drum improvisation by Baby
   Dodds **C** Merce Cunningham
   FP Hunter Playhouse, New York

*The Princess Zondilda and
Her Entourage*
"A Theatrical Fantasy by Merce
   Cunningham" **M** Alexei Haieff
   - **S, C** Merce Cunningham **FP** Hunter
   Playhouse, New York

1946

1947

The Seasons
Ballet in one act, divided into nine sections
   M John Cage **S, C** Isamu Noguchi
   FP Ballet Society, Ziegfeld Theater,
   New York

The Open Road
Solo **M** Lou Harrison **C** Merce
   Cunningham **FP** Hunter Playhouse,
   New York

Dromenon
   M John Cage **C** for Merce Cunningham:
   Sonja Sekula; for women: Merce
   Cunningham **FP** Hunter Playhouse,
   New York

Dream
Solo **M** John Cage **C** Merce Cunningham
   FP Stephens College, Columbia,
   Missouri

The Ruse of Medusa
A lyric comedy in one act by Erik Satie,
   translated from the French by M. C.
   Richards **M** Erik Satie Directed by
   Helen Livingston and Arthur Penn
   Dances by Merce Cunningham
   S Willem and Elaine de Kooning
   C Mary Outten **FP** Black Mountain
   College, Black Mountain, North
   Carolina

A Diversion
   M John Cage **C** for Merce Cunningham:
   himself; for women: Mary Outten
   FP Black Mountain College, Black
   Mountain, North Carolina

Orestes
Solo **M** (sometimes performed in silence)
   John Cage **C** Merce Cunningham
   FP Black Mountain College, Black
   Mountain, North Carolina

[The] Monkey Dances
Solo in seven parts **M** Erik Satie **C** Mary
   Outten; tail by Richard Lippold, hat by
   Merce Cunningham **FP** Black
   Mountain College, Black Mountain,
   North Carolina

1948

1949

Effusions Avant L'heure
   M John Cage **C** practice clothes
   FP Jean Hélion's Studio, Paris

Amores
   M John Cage **C** practice clothes
   FP Jean Hélion's Studio, Paris

Duet
   M unknown **C** Léonor Fini **FP** at a garden
   fête, Paris

Two Step
Solo **M** Erik Satie **C** Merce Cunningham
   FP New York City Dance Theater, City
   Center, New York

Pool of Darkness
   M Ben Weber **C** Merce Cunningham
   FP Hunter Playhouse, New York

Before Dawn
Solo **M** (in silence) **C** Merce Cunningham
   FP Hunter Playhouse, New York

Waltz
   M Erik Satie **FP** Student Group, Louisiana
   State University, Baton Rouge, Louisiana

Rag-Time Parade
   M Erik Satie **C** from thrift shops
   FP Student Group, Louisiana State
   University, Baton Rouge, Louisiana

Waltz
Solo **M** Erik Satie **FP** Cooper Union,
   New York

1950

1951

*Sixteen Dances for Soloist and
Company of Three*
In sixteen parts **M** John Cage **C**, Properties:
   Eleanor de Vito, John Cage, Remy
   Charlip, Merce Cunningham; coat a
   gift from Antoinette Larrabee and
   Constance Smith; mask by Remy
   Charlip after a sketch by John Heliker
   FP Bennett Junior College, Millbrook,
   New York

Variation
Solo **M** Morton Feldman **C** Merce
   Cunningham **FP** University of
   Washington, Seattle

Boy Who Wanted to Be a Bird
Solo **M** (in silence) **FP** Martha's Vineyard,
   Massachusetts

Merce Cunningham in Sixteen Dances for
Soloist and Company of Three
Photo: Gerda Peterich

Suite by Chance
In four movements **M** Christian Wolff
   C Remy Charlip **FP** (preview) Dancers
   Studio, New York

Suite of Six Short Dances
Solo **M** recorder pieces, arranged by W. P.
   Jennerjahn **FP** Black Mountain College,
   Black Mountain, North Carolina

*Excerpts from Symphonie pour
un homme seul*
In two parts **M** Pierre Schaeffer, with the
   collaboration of Pierre Henry **C** street
   clothes **FP** Festival of the Creative Arts,
   Brandeis University, Waltham,
   Massachusetts

Les Noces
"A Choral Ballet in four scenes" **M** and
   text Igor Stravinsky **S, C** Howard Bay
   FP Festival of the Creative Arts, Brandeis
   University, Waltham, Massachusetts

Brigadoon
Musical play in three (originally two) acts
   Book and lyrics by Alan Jay Lerner
   M Frederick Loewe Dances by Merce
   Cunningham **S** Barrie Greenbie
   C Ruth Young **FP** Burnsville School of
   the Arts, Parkway Playhouse, Burnsville,
   North Carolina

[Theatre Piece]
Performed by John Cage, Nicola Cernovich,
   Merce Cunningham, Charles Olson,
   Robert Rauschenberg **M** C. Richards,
   David Tudor **FP** Black Mountain
   College, Black Mountain, North Carolina

1952

1953

Solo Suite in Space and Time
Solo in five parts **M** John Cage **C** Merce
   Cunningham **FP** Louisiana State
   University, Baton Rouge

Demonstration Piece
In four movements **M** (in silence)
   FP Student Group, Louisiana State
   University, Baton Rouge

Epilogue
   M Erik Satie **FP** Student Group, Louisiana
   State University, Baton Rouge

Banjo
   M Louis Moreau Gottschalk **C** Remy
   Charlip **FP** MCDC, Black Mountain
   College, Black Mountain, North Carolina

Dime a Dance
   M "The Whole World," a program of nine-
   teenth-century piano music selected by
   David Tudor **C** Remy Charlip
   FP MCDC, Black Mountain College,
   Black Mountain, North Carolina

Septet
   M Erik Satie **C** Remy Charlip
   FP MCDC, Black Mountain College,
   Black Mountain, North Carolina

Untitled Solo*
Solo **M** Christian Wolff **C** Merce
   Cunningham **FP** MCDC, Black
   Mountain College, Black Mountain,
   North Carolina *Called Solo at first
   performance

Fragments
In three parts, the second in silence
   M Pierre Boulez **C** Remy Charlip
   FP MCDC, Theater de Lys, New York

Merce Cunningham and Remy Charlip in
Antic Meet Photo: Matthew Wysocki

Galaxy
"A quartet of solos" **M** Earle Brown
    C Remy Charlip **FP** MCDC, University
    of Notre Dame, South Bend, Indiana

Lavish Escapade
Solo **M** Christian Wolff **C** Merce
    Cunningham **FP** MCDC, University
    of Notre Dame, South Bend, Indiana

Suite for Five in Space and Time
In eight parts **M** John Cage **C** Robert
    Rauschenberg **FP** MCDC, University
    of Notre Dame, South Bend, Indiana

Nocturnes
In five parts, _"from dusk to the witching
    hour"_ **M** Erik Satie **S,C** Robert
    Rauschenberg **FP** MCDC, Jacob's
    Pillow, Lee, Massachusetts

Antic Meet
In nine parts **M** John Cage **C** and properties
    by Robert Rauschenberg **FP** MCDC,
    Eleventh American Dance Festival,
    Connecticut College, New London,
    Connecticut

Summerspace
A Lyric Dance **M** Morton Feldman
    S,C Robert Rauschenberg
    FP MCDC, Eleventh American Dance
    Festival, Connecticut College, New
    London, Connecticut

Nattvandrare (Night Wandering)
M Bo Nilsson **C** Nicola Cernovich
    FP Merce Cunningham and Carolyn
    Brown, Kungl Teatern, Stockholm,
    Sweden

Theatre Piece
M John Cage **FP** Composers' Showcase,
    Circle in the Square, New York

The Cook's Quadrille
A show for children by Juliette Waung,
    Steve Paxton, Julia Hurd, and Bernice
    Mendelsohn Duet **M** Merce
    Cunningham (tape) Dances by Merce
    Cunningham **FP** The Living Theatre,
    New York

Crises
M Conlon Nancarrow **C** Robert
    Rauschenberg **FP** MCDC, Thirteenth
    American Dance Festival, Connecticut
    College, New London, Connecticut

Hands Birds
Solo **M** Earle Brown **C** Robert
    Rauschenberg **FP** Carolyn Brown,
    Venice Biennale, XXIII Festival
    Internazionale di Musica
    Contemporanea, Teatro la Fenice,
    Venice

Waka
Solo **M** Toshi Ichiyanagi **C** Robert
    Rauschenberg (from The Poems of
    White Stone) **FP** Carolyn Brown,
    Venice Biennale, XXIII Festival
    Internazionale di Musica
    Contemporanea, Teatro la Fenice,
    Venice

Music Walk with Dancers
M John Cage **FP** Merce Cunningham and
    Carolyn Brown, Venice Biennale, XXIII
    Festival Internazionale di Musica
    Contemporanea, Teatro la Fenice,
    Venice

Minutiae
M John Cage **S** Robert Rauschenberg
    C Remy Charlip **FP** MCDC, Brooklyn
    Academy of Music, Brooklyn, New York

1954

1956

1958

1960

1955

Springweather and People
M Earle Brown **C** Remy Charlip, with the
    collaboration of Robert Rauschenberg,
    Ray Johnson, and Vera Williams
    FP MCDC, Bard College, Annandale-
    on-Hudson, New York

The Young Disciple
"A martyrology in three acts," by Paul
    Goodman Directed and designed by
    Julian Beck **M** Pierre Schaeffer, with the
    collaboration of Pierre Henry and Ned
    Rorem Dances by Merce Cunningham
    FP The Living Theatre, New York

1957

Labyrinthian Dances
"area without exit" In four parts **M** Josef
    Matthias Hauer **S, C** Robert
    Rauschenberg **FP** MCDC, Brooklyn
    Academy of Music, Brooklyn, New York

Changeling
Solo **M** Christian Wolff **C** Robert
    Rauschenberg **FP** MCDC, Brooklyn
    Academy of Music, Brooklyn, New York

Picnic Polka
M Louis Moreau Gottschalk **C** Remy
    Charlip **FP** MCDC, Brooklyn Academy
    of Music, Brooklyn, New York

1959

From the Poems of White Stone
M Chou Wen-Chung, with poems by
    Chiang Kuei (circa 1155–1221 A.D.)
    C Robert Rauschenberg **FP** MCDC,
    University of Illinois, Urbana

Gambit for Dancers and Orchestra
In six parts **M** Ben Johnston **C** and projection
    by Robert Rauschenberg **FP** MCDC,
    University of Illinois, Urbana

The Cave at Machpelah
Play in three acts by Paul Goodman
    Directed and designed by Julian Beck
    Dances by Merce Cunningham
    M Ned Rorem **FP** The Living Theatre,
    New York

Rune
M Christian Wolff **C** Robert Rauschenberg
    FP MCDC, Twelfth American Dance
    Festival, Connecticut College, New
    London, Connecticut

1961

Suite de Danses
Dance for television **M** Serge Garrant
    C Jasper Johns Directed by Jean
    Mercure MCDC, filmed for Société
    Radio-Canada, "Sérénade Estivale,"
    Montréal

Aeon
M John Cage **C** and objects Robert
    Rauschenberg **FP** MCDC, Montréal
    Festival, La Comédie Canadienne,
    Montréal

1962

The Construction of Boston
A collaboration by Niki de Saint-Phalle, Robert Rauschenberg, Jean Tinguely, and Kenneth Koch (text) Directed by Merce Cunningham **FP** Maidman Theatre, New York

1963

Field Dances
M John Cage **C** Robert Rauschenberg **FP** MCDC, University of California, Los Angeles

Story
M Toshi Ichiyanagi **S,C** Robert Rauschenberg **FP** MCDC, University of California, Los Angeles

1964

Open Session
Solo **M** (in silence) **C** Merce Cunningham **FP** MCDC, Wadsworth Atheneum, Hartford, Connecticut

Paired
M John Cage **C** Robert Rauschenberg **FP** MCDC, Wadsworth Atheneum, Hartford, Connecticut

Winterbranch
M La Monte Young **C** and object Robert Rauschenberg **FP** MCDC, Wadsworth Atheneum, Hartford, Connecticut

*Museum Event #1**
M John Cage **C** and properties: Robert Rauschenberg **FP** MCDC, Museum des 20. Jahrhunderts, Vienna *This was the first *Event* performance by Merce Cunningham Dance Company; the hundreds of subsequent *Events* are not listed in this chronology.

Cross Currents
M Conlon Nancarrow, arranged by John Cage **C** Merce Cunningham **FP** MCDC, Sadler's Wells Theatre, London

1965

Variations V
M John Cage Film: Stan VanDerBeek Distortion of video images: Nam June Paik **C** street and practice clothes **FP** MCDC, French-American Festival, Philharmonic Hall, New York Film version made in Hamburg in 1966; produced by Studio Hamburg; directed by Arne Arnbom

How to Pass, Kick, Fall and Run
M John Cage **FP** MCDC, Harper Theatre, Chicago

Merce Cunningham and John Cage on the set of Variations V Photo: Hervé Gloaguen

1966

Place
M Gordon Mumma **S,C** Beverly Emmons **FP** MCDC, Fondation Maeght, Saint-Paul de Vence, France

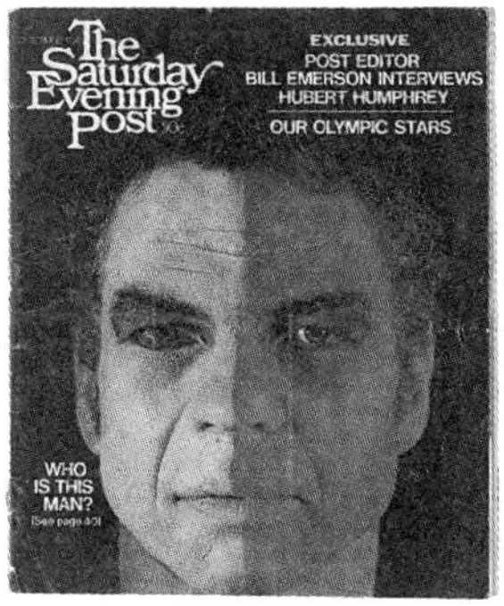

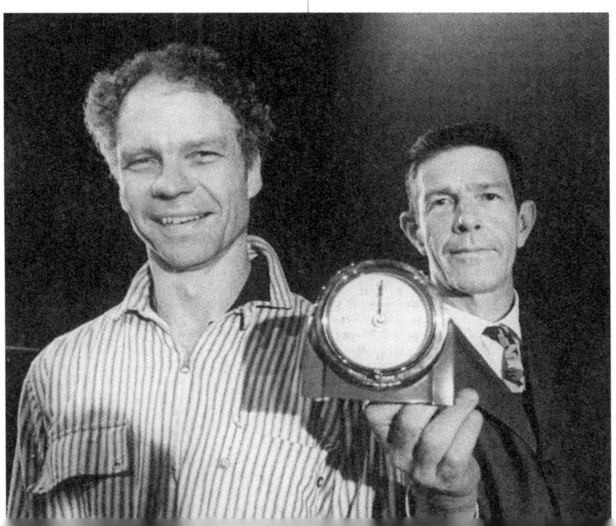

1967

Scramble
M Toshi Ichiyanagi **S,C** Frank Stella **FP** MCDC, Ravinia Festival, Chicago

1968

Merce Cunningham on the cover of The Saturday Evening Post, October 19, 1968

RainForest
M David Tudor **S** Andy Warhol (Silver Clouds) **C** Jasper Johns **FP** MCDC, 2nd Buffalo Festival of the Arts Today, State University College at Buffalo, New York

Walkaround Time
M David Behrman **S** after Marcel Duchamp's Large Glass, supervised by Jasper Johns **C** Jasper Johns **FP** MCDC, 2nd Buffalo Festival of the Arts Today, State University College at Buffalo, New York

Assemblage
A film for television Directed by Richard Moore **M** John Cage, David Tudor, Gordon Mumma **FP** MCDC, KQED-TV, San Francisco Original working title: Ghirardelli Square

1969

Canfield
M Pauline Oliveros **S** Robert Morris **C** Jasper Johns (uncredited) **FP** MCDC, Nazareth College, Rochester, New York

Merce Cunningham in <u>TV Rerun</u>
Photo: Jack Mitchell

Tread
M Christian Wolff **S** Bruce Nauman
   C Merce Cunningham **FP** MCDC,
   Brooklyn Academy of Music, Brooklyn,
   New York

Second Hand
In three parts **M** John Cage **C** Jasper Johns
   FP MCDC, Brooklyn Academy of
   Music, Brooklyn, New York

Signals
M David Tudor, Gordon Mumma,
   John Cage **C** Merce Cunningham
   FP MCDC, Théâtre de France, Paris

Objects
M Alvin Lucier **S** Neil Jenney **FP** MCDC,
   Brooklyn Academy of Music, Brooklyn,
   New York

1971

Loops
<u>Event</u> for soloist **M** Gordon Mumma, per-
   formed in front of Jasper Johns' <u>Map</u>
   (based on Buckminster Fuller's
   <u>Dymaxion Air Ocean World</u>) Slides by
   Charles Atlas **FP** The Museum of
   Modern Art, New York

Landrover
In four parts **M** John Cage, Gordon
   Mumma, David Tudor **C** Jasper Johns
   FP MCDC, Brooklyn Academy of
   Music, Brooklyn, New York

TV Rerun
M Gordon Mumma **S,C** Jasper Johns
   FP MCDC, Brooklyn Academy of
   Music, Brooklyn, New York

Borst Park
M Christian Wolff **C** The Company
   FP MCDC, Brooklyn Academy of
   Music, Brooklyn, New York

1973

Changing Steps
M David Behrman, John Cage, Gordon
   Mumma, David Tudor **C** Charles Atlas
   FP MCDC, as part of <u>Event #65</u>,
   Brooklyn Academy of Music, Brooklyn,
   New York Video version directed by
   Elliot Caplan and Merce Cunningham
   M John Cage **C** Mark Lancaster, Suzanne
   Gallo First public screening at Anthology
   Film Archives, New York, 1989

Un Jour ou Deux
M John Cage **S,C** Jasper Johns, assisted by
   Mark Lancaster **FP** Ballet de l'Opéra
   de Paris, Salle Garnier, Paris

Westbeth
A work for video, directed by Charles Atlas
   and Merce Cunningham **M** John Cage
   C Mark Lancaster, from a design by
   Jasper Johns (for <u>Un Jour ou Deux</u>,
   1973) First public showing following a
   live performance of the dance, Merce
   Cunningham Studio, Westbeth, New
   York, 1975

1975

Exercise Piece
C Mark Lancaster **FP** MCDC, Merce
   Cunningham Studio, Westbeth,
   New York

Rebus
M David Behrman **S,C** Mark Lancaster
   FP MCDC, Music Hall, Detroit,
   Michigan

Sounddance
M David Tudor **S,C** Mark Lancaster
   FP MCDC, Music Hall, Detroit,
   Michigan

Solo
Solo **M** John Cage **C** Sonja Sekula (from
   <u>Dromenon</u>, 1947) **FP** MCDC, Music
   Hall, Detroit, Michigan

Blue Studio: Five Segments
Solo Videotape by Merce Cunningham and
   Charles Atlas, WNET/TV Lab

Torse
In three parts **M** Maryanne Amacher
   C Mark Lancaster **FP** MCDC,
   McCarter Theatre, Princeton,
   New Jersey Film version directed by
   Charles Atlas

Squaregame
M Takehisa Kosugi **S,C** Mark Lancaster
   FP MCDC, Festival Theatre, Adelaide,
   Australia

Video Triangle
M David Tudor **C** Mark Lancaster
   Videotaped with MCDC as part of
   <u>Event for Television</u>, WNET <u>Dance in
   America</u> series, directed by Merrill
   Brockway in Nashville, Tennessee

1977

Travelogue
M John Cage **S,C** Robert Rauschenberg
   (<u>Tantric Geography</u>) **FP** MCDC,
   Minskoff Theater, New York

Inlets
M John Cage **S,C** Morris Graves, realized
   by Suzanne Joelson **FP** MCDC,
   University of Washington, Seattle,
   Washington

Fractions I
A work for video, directed by Charles Atlas
   and Merce Cunningham **M** Jon Gibson
   S,C Mark Lancaster

Merce Cunningham (left) and Charles Atlas
filming Locale   Photo: Art Becofsky

Exercise Piece I
M Meredith Monk **C** Suzanne Joelson
FP MCDC, as part of Event #215,
Roundabout Theatre, New York

Exercise Piece II
In two parts **M** John Cage **C** Mark
Lancaster **FP** MCDC, as part of
Changing Steps et cetera, Royal
Alexandra Theatre, Toronto

Exchange
M David Tudor **S,C** Jasper Johns
FP MCDC, City Center Theater, New
York Filmed by Charles Atlas 1978;
film stock unedited

Tango
Solo **M** John Cage **S,C** Mark Lancaster
FP MCDC, City Center Theater,
New York

1978

1979

Locale
Filmdance, directed by Charles Atlas
and Merce Cunningham **M** Takehisa
Kosugi **C** Charles Atlas First public
screening, City Center Theater, New
York, 1980

Roadrunners
M Yasunao Tone **C** Mark Lancaster
FP MCDC, American Dance Festival,
Duke University, Durham,
North Carolina

Exercise Piece III
M John Cage **C** Mark Lancaster
FP MCDC, City Center Theater,
New York

Duets
M Peadar and Mel Mercier (percussion
arranged by John Cage and John
Fullemann) **C** Mark Lancaster
FP MCDC, City Center Theater,
New York

Fielding Sixes
M John Cage, with musicians Paddy
Glackin and Matt Molloy **S,C** Monika
Fullemann **FP** MCDC, Sadler's Wells
Theatre, London

1980

1981

Channels/Inserts
Filmdance, directed by Charles Atlas and
Merce Cunningham **M** David Tudor
C Charles Atlas First public screening,
Carnegie Hall Cinema, New York, 1982

10's with Shoes
M Martin Kalve **S,C** Mark Lancaster
FP MCDC, City Center Theater,
New York

Gallopade
In six parts **M** Takehisa Kosugi **C** Mark
Lancaster **FP** MCDC, Théâtre de
Beaulieu, Lausanne

Channels/Inserts

Trails
M John Cage **S,C** Mark Lancaster
FP MCDC, City Center Theater,
New York

Numbers
Event material, in three parts **FP** MCDC,
City Center Theater, New York

Quartet
M David Tudor **C** Mark Lancaster
FP MCDC, Grand Casino de Génève,
Geneva

1982

1983

Coast Zone
Filmdance, directed by Charles Atlas and
Merce Cunningham **M** Larry Austin
C Mark Lancaster and Charles Atlas
First public screenings: Dean Junior
College, Franklin, Massachusetts; Merce
Cunningham Studio, Westbeth, New
York, 1984

Inlets 2
M John Cage **C** Mark Lancaster
FP MCDC, Festival de Lille, Le Colisée,
Roubaix, France

Roaratorio
"An Irish circus on Finnegans Wake"
M John Cage Text by John Cage, drawn
from Finnegans Wake by James Joyce
C Mark Lancaster **FP** MCDC, Festival
de Lille, Le Colisée, Roubaix, France

Pictures
M David Behrman **S,C** Mark Lancaster
FP MCDC, City Center Theater,
New York

Doubles
M Takehisa Kosugi **S,C** Mark Lancaster
FP MCDC, American Dance
Festival, Duke University, Durham,
North Carolina

Phrases
M David Tudor **S** William Anastasi
C Dove Bradshaw **FP** MCDC, Théâtre
Municipal d'Angers, France

1984

1985

Deli Commedia
Videodance, directed by Elliot Caplan
M Pat Richter **C** Dove Bradshaw

Native Green
M John King **S,C** William Anastasi
FP MCDC, City Center Theater,
New York

Arcade
M John Cage **S,C** Dove Bradshaw
FP Pennsylvania Ballet, Academy
of Music, Philadelphia, Pennsylvania

MC

Grange Eve
M Takehisa Kosugi **S,C** William Anastasi
FP MCDC, City Center Theater,
New York

Points in Space
Videodance, directed by Elliot Caplan and
Merce Cunningham **M** John Cage
S William Anastasi **C** Dove Bradshaw
First public screening, Herbst Theatre,
San Francisco, 1986

164   **1986**

1987

Fabrications
M Emanuel Dimas de Melo Pimenta
S,C Dove Bradshaw Co-commissioned
and copresented by the Walker Art
Center and Northrop Auditorium
FP MCDC, Northrop Auditorium,
Minneapolis

Shards
M David Tudor **S,C** William Anastasi
FP MCDC, City Center Theater,
New York

Carousal
M Takehisa Kosugi **C** Dove Bradshaw
FP MCDC, Jacob's Pillow, Lee,
Massachusetts

Eleven
M Robert Ashley **C** William Anastasi
FP MCDC, Joyce Theater, New York

Five Stone
M John Cage, David Tudor **S,C** Mark
Lancaster **FP** MCDC, Freie
Wolksbühne Berlin, Berlin

Five Stone Wind
M John Cage, Takehisa Kosugi, David Tudor
S,C Mark Lancaster **FP** MCDC, The
Plaza, World Financial Center, New York

1988

1989

Cargo X
M Takehisa Kosugi **C** Dove Bradshaw
FP MCDC, University of Texas, Austin

Field and Figures
M Ivan Tcherepnin **S,C** Kristin Jones and
Andrew Ginzel Co-commissioned and
copresented by the Walker Art Center
and Northrop Auditorium **FP** MCDC,
Northrop Auditorium, Minneapolis

Inventions
M John Cage **S,C** Carl Kielblock
FP MCDC, Théâtre Antique, Arles,
France (preview without decor; per-
formed in costumes by Mark Lancaster)

August Pace
M Michael Pugliese **S,C** Afrika (Sergei
Bugaev) **FP** MCDC, University of
California, Berkeley

Polarity
M David Tudor **S** William Anastasi, from
drawings by Merce Cunningham
C William Anastasi **FP** MCDC,
City Center Theater, New York

Walking Dance
FP MCDC, Teatro Pérez Galdós, Las
Palmas, Canarias, as part of one of four
Events Canarias

Walkaround Time Falls
FP MCDC, Damrosch Park, Lincoln
Center, New York, as part of an Event
for Lincoln Center Out-of-Doors

Four Lifts
FP MCDC, Théâtre National Populaire,
Villeurbanne, France, as part of Event 1,
4ème Biennale de la Danse, Lyon

1990

1991

Neighbors
M Takehisa Kosugi **S,C** Mark Lancaster
FP MCDC, City Center Theater,
New York

Trackers
M Emanuel Dimas de Melo Pimenta
S,C Dove Bradshaw **FP** MCDC, City
Center Theater, New York

Beach Birds
M John Cage **C** Marsha Skinner
FP MCDC, Theater 11, Zürich Film
version under the title Beach Birds For
Camera, directed by Elliot Caplan

Loosestrife
M Michael Pugliese **S,C** Carl Kielblock
FP MCDC, Théâtre de la Ville, Paris

Change of Address
M Walter Zimmermann **S,C** Marsha
Skinner **FP** MCDC, University of
Texas, Austin

Touchbase
M Michael Pugliese **S,C** Mark Lancaster
FP Rambert Dance Company, Royalty
Theatre, London

Enter
M David Tudor **S,C** Marsha Skinner;
backdrop and costume photography
from a video still by Elliot Caplan;
Rideau de scène (backdrop): John Cage
FP MCDC, Opéra de Paris Garnier, Paris

1992

1993

Doubletoss
M Takehisa Kosugi **S** Merce Cunningham,
with Aaron Copp **C** Merce Cunningham,
with Suzanne Gallo Co-commissioned
and copresented by the Walker Art
Center and Northrop Auditorium
FP MCDC, Northrop Auditorium,
Minneapolis

CRWDSPCR
M John King **S,C** Mark Lancaster
FP MCDC, American Dance Festival,
Duke University, Durham,
Noth Carolina

Beach Birds
Photo: Jack Vartoogian

David Tudor

Breakers
M John Driscoll **S,C** Mary Jean Kenton **FP** MCDC, City Center Theater, New York

Ocean
Concept by John Cage and Merce Cunningham **M** Andrew Culver, David Tudor **S,C** Marsha Skinner **FP** MCDC, kunstenFESTIVALdesArts, Cirque Royal, Brussels

4'33"
Ch The Company **M** John Cage **C** street clothes **FP** MCDC, Central Park SummerStage, New York

1994

1995

The Slouch
Event material **FP** MCDC, in a MinEvent at City Center Theater, New York

Ground Level Overlay
M Stuart Dempster **S** Leonardo Drew **C** Suzanne Gallo **FP** MCDC, City Center Theater, New York

Windows
M Emanuel Dimas de Melo Pimenta **S** after an etching by John Cage (Global Village 1–36, 1989) **C** Suzanne Gallo **FP** MCDC Montpellier Danse 95, Opéra Berlioz, Le Corum, Montpellier, France

Tune In/Spin Out
M John Cage **C** Suzanne Gallo and Merce Cunningham **FP** MCDC, University of Texas, Austin

Installations
M Trimpin **S** video installation by Elliot Caplan **C** Elliot Caplan and Suzanne Gallo **FP** MCDC, Meany Theater, University of Washington, Seattle

Rondo
In two parts **M** John Cage **C** Suzanne Gallo and Merce Cunningham **FP** MCDC, Ludwigsburger Schlossfestspiele, Theater im Forum, Ludwigsburg, Germany

1996

1997

Scenario
M Takehisa Kosugi **C** Rei Kawakubo **S** Takao Kawasaki **FP** MCDC, Brooklyn Academy of Music, Brooklyn, New York

Pond Way
M Brian Eno **S** Roy Lichtenstein (Landscape with Boat, 1996) **C** Suzanne Gallo **FP** MCDC, Opéra National de Paris, Palais Garnier, Paris

1998

Merce Cunningham   Photo: Atsushi Iijima

Abbreviations:

C Costumes by
FP First performance
M Music by

Unless otherwise noted, music, choreography, and direction by Meredith Monk; all films and videos directed by Meredith Monk unless specified.

EARLY WORK

And Sarah Knew 1962
For five performers **M** Israeli folk music
FP Sarah Lawrence College, Bronxville, New York

Troubadour Songs 1963
For three performers **M** Medieval French music **FP** Sarah Lawrence College, Bronxville, New York

Vibrato 1963
For four performers **M** William Schuman
FP Sarah Lawrence College, Bronxville, New York

Timestop 1964
For five performers **FP** Sarah Lawrence College, Bronxville, New York

Untitled 1964
For two performers **M** Daniel Pinkham
FP Sarah Lawrence College, Bronxville, New York

Diploid 1964
For two performers **M** Collaboration with Elizabeth Keen **FP** Clark Center for the Performing Arts, New York

Arm's Length 1964
For six performers **M** sound collage
FP Sarah Lawrence College, Bronxville, New York

Cowell Suite 1964
Solo **M** Henry Cowell **FP** Sarah Lawrence College, Bronxville, New York

Break 1964
Solo, tape collage **FP** Washington Square Galleries, New York

Cartoon 1965
For seven performers **FP** Judson Memorial Church, New York

The Beach 1965
Solo with tape collage **FP** Hardware Poets Playhouse, New York

Relâche 1965
In collaboration with Dick Higgins. For six performers **M** Erik Satie **FP** Judson Hall, New York

Blackboard 1965
Solo **FP** Judson Hall, New York

Radar 1965
For two performers **FP** Judson Hall, New York

Portable 1966
For two performers **FP** Judson Memorial Church, New York

Duet with Cat's Scream and Locomotive 1966
For two performers with tape collage
FP The Gate Theater, New York

MUSICAL COMPOSITIONS/RECORDINGS
16 Millimeter Earrings
Voice, guitar, tapes

OPERAS/MUSICAL THEATER/ SITE-SPECIFIC WORKS
16 Millimeter Earrings
Solo incorporating film **FP** Judson Memorial Church, New York

1966

1967

MUSICAL COMPOSITIONS/RECORDINGS
Candy Bullets and Moon
In collaboration with Don Preston. Voice, electric organ, electric bass, drums; released as a single, out of print; re-released on Better an Old Demon Than a New God (1984), Giorno Poetry Systems records, GPS 033

Dying Swan with Sunglasses
Solo voice with echoplex and tape

OPERAS/MUSICAL THEATER/ SITE-SPECIFIC WORKS
Blueprint
For twelve performers **FP** Group 212, Woodstock, New York

Overload
For four performers **FP** Expo '67, Montreal

Overload/Blueprint 2
For five performers **FP** in two parts: Judson Gallery and Judson Memorial Church, New York

FILMS/VIDEOS
Children
Black-and-white, silent, 16mm, 9 minutes Camera by Phil Niblock

16 Millimeter Earrings
Photo: Charlotte Victoria

OPERAS/MUSICAL THEATER/ SITE-SPECIFIC WORKS
Blueprint (3)
For three performers **FP** Colby College, Waterville, Maine

Blueprint (4)
For two performers **FP** The House Loft, New York

Blueprint (5)
For eight performers **FP** Julius Tobias Studio, New York

Co-op
For approximately thirty performers
FP Loeb Student Center, New York University, New York

FILMS/VIDEOS
Ballbearing
Color, silent, 16mm, 6½- and 13-minute loops that play continuously forward and backward Camera by Meredith Monk and George Landow

1968

1969

MUSICAL COMPOSITIONS/RECORDINGS
Juice: a theatre cantata in 3 installments
Eighty-five voices, Jew's harp, two violins

OPERAS/MUSICAL THEATER/ SITE-SPECIFIC WORKS
Juice: a theatre cantata in 3 installments
For eighty-five performers **FP** in New York at three sites: The Solomon R. Guggenheim Museum; The Minor Latham Playhouse, Barnard College; and The House Loft

Tour: Dedicated to Dinosaurs
For sixty performers **FP** Smithsonian Institution, Washington, D.C.

Tour 2: Barbershop
For sixty-five performers **FP** Museum of Contemporary Art, Chicago

Tour 3: Lounge
For fifty performers **FP** Alfred University, Alfred, New York

MUSICAL COMPOSITIONS/RECORDINGS
Key: An Album of Invisible Theater
Solo voice and electric organ, vocal quartet, percussion, Jew's harp; released on Increase Records; re-released on Lovely Music, Ltd. (1977), LML 1051

OPERAS/MUSICAL THEATER/ SITE-SPECIFIC WORKS
A Raw Recital
Solo **FP** Whitney Museum of American Art, New York

Needle-Brain Lloyd and the Systems Kid: a live movie
For one hundred fifty performers
FP American Dance Festival, in four sites at Connecticut College, New London, Connecticut

Tour 4: Organ
For sixty performers **FP** Douglas College, New Brunswick, New Jersey

Tour 5: Glass
For fifty performers **FP** Nazareth College, Rochester, New York

Tour 6: Gym
For twelve performers **FP** Auburn Community College, Auburn, New York

Tour 7: Factory
For fifteen performers **FP** State University of New York, Buffalo

1970

1971

MUSICAL COMPOSITIONS/RECORDINGS
Plainsong for Bill's Bojo
Electric organ

Vessel: an opera epic
Seventy-five voices, electric organ, dulcimer, accordion

OPERAS/MUSICAL THEATER/ SITE-SPECIFIC WORKS
Tour 8: Castle
For approximately seventy performers
FP at four sites: Milwaukee and Stevens Point, Wisconsin; Holland and Marquette, Michigan

Vessel: an opera epic
For seventy-five performers **FP** in New York at three sites: The House Loft, The Performing Garage, and Wooster Parking Lot

FILMS/VIDEOS
Mountain
Color, silent, 16mm, 10 minutes Camera by Robin Lloyd

MUSICAL COMPOSITIONS/RECORDINGS

Biography
Solo voice, piano

Paris
Solo piano

Our Lady of Late
Solo voice, wine glass

**OPERAS/MUSICAL THEATER/
SITE-SPECIFIC WORKS**

*Education of the Girlchild:
an opera (Part 1)*
Solo voice, piano **FP** International Theatre
Festival, Nancy, France

Paris
In collaboration with Ping Chong. For
three performers **FP** The House Loft,
New York

1972

1973

**OPERAS/MUSICAL THEATER/
SITE-SPECIFIC WORKS**

*Education of the Girlchild:
an opera*
For thirteen performers **FP** Common
Ground Theater, New York

MUSICAL COMPOSITIONS/RECORDINGS

Our Lady of Late
Solo voice, wine glass, percussion
Released on Minona Records, out of print

**OPERAS/MUSICAL THEATER/
SITE-SPECIFIC WORKS**

Chacon
In collaboration with Ping Chong. For
twenty-five performers **FP** Oberlin
College, Oberlin, Ohio

1974

1975

MUSICAL COMPOSITIONS/RECORDINGS

Small Scroll
Solo voice, piano, soprano recorder

**OPERAS/MUSICAL THEATER/
SITE-SPECIFIC WORKS**

Anthology and Small Scroll
For nine performers **FP** St. Mark's Church,
New York

FILMS/VIDEOS

Quarry
Black-and-white, silent, 16mm, 5 minutes.
Camera and editing by David Gearey;
for projection during the opera Quarry

LA BIENNALE
Un laboratorio internazionale

Publication for the 1975 Venice Biennale,
featuring Education of the Girlchild

MUSICAL COMPOSITIONS/RECORDINGS

Quarry: an opera
Thirty-eight voices, two pump organs, two
soprano recorders, tape

Venice/Milan
Fifteen voices, piano four-hands

Songs from the Hill
Unaccompanied solo voice

Tablet
Four voices, piano four hands, two soprano
recorders

**OPERAS/MUSICAL THEATER/
SITE-SPECIFIC WORKS**

Quarry: an opera
For forty performers **FP** La Mama Annex,
New York

Venice-Milan
In collaboration with Ping Chong. For
twelve performers **FP** Washington
Project for the Arts, Washington, D.C.

1976

1977

MUSICAL COMPOSITIONS/RECORDINGS

Rally; Procession on Airwaves
Twenty-eight voices; solo voice and piano
Released on One Ten Records, OTOO1/2

**OPERAS/MUSICAL THEATER/
SITE-SPECIFIC WORKS**

Tablet
For eight performers **FP** MOMING,
Chicago

The Travelogue Series
For thirty performers **FP** The Roundabout
Theater, New York

FILMS/VIDEOS

Home Movie Circa 1910
Black-and-white, silent, Super-8 and 16mm,
5 minutes. Camera by Meredith Monk;
edited by Meredith Monk and Tony
Janetti; shown in Ping Chong's
Humboldt's Current

MUSICAL COMPOSITIONS/RECORDINGS

Biography on Big Ego
Solo voice and piano; released on Giorno
Poetry Systems Records, GPS 0112-013

**OPERAS/MUSICAL THEATER/
SITE-SPECIFIC WORKS**

The Plateau Series
For eight performers **FP** St. Mark's Church,
New York

FILMS/VIDEOS

Quarry
Color, sound, 16mm, 86 minutes. Produced
by Amram Nowak Associates; a documentary record of the opera, performed
by The House Company

1978

1979

MUSICAL COMPOSITIONS/RECORDINGS

Dolmen Music
Six voices, cello, percussion **FP** The
Kitchen, New York

Songs from the Hill/Tablet
Four voices, piano four hands, two soprano
recorders; released on Wergo Records,
SM 1022

Recent Ruins
Fourteen voices, tape, cello

**OPERAS/MUSICAL THEATER/
SITE-SPECIFIC WORKS**

Recent Ruins
For fourteen performers **FP** La Mama
Annex, New York

FILMS/VIDEOS

Ellis Island
Black-and-white, silent, 16mm, 7 minutes.
Associate Director Bob Rosen; camera
by Jerry Pantzer; made for screening
during a performance of Recent Ruins

1980

**OPERAS/MUSICAL THEATER/
SITE-SPECIFIC WORKS**
*Vessel: an opera epic
(Berlin version)*
For eighty performers **FP** in West Berlin at
three locations: S.O. 36, Schaubühne am
Lehniner Platz, and Anhalter Bahnhof

FILMS/VIDEOS
16 Millimeter Earrings
Color, sound, 16mm, 25 minutes. Produced,
directed, and photographed by Robert
Withers; conceived and performed by
Meredith Monk

1981

MUSICAL COMPOSITIONS/RECORDINGS
Dolmen Music
Six voices, piano, violin, cello, percussion.
Released on ECM New Series, CD, 78118-
21197-2

Turtle Dreams (Waltz)
Four voices, two electric organs

Specimen Days
Fourteen voices, piano, two electric organs

**OPERAS/MUSICAL THEATER/
SITE-SPECIFIC WORKS**
Music Concert with Film
For eight performers **FP** The Space at City
Center, New York

Specimen Days: a civil war opera
For fifteen performers **FP** The Public
Theater, New York

FILMS/VIDEOS
Ellis Island
Color and black-and-white, sound, 35mm
and videotape, 28 minutes Produced by
Bob Rosen Codirected by Meredith
Monk and Bob Rose Camera by Jerry
Pantzer

1982

MUSICAL COMPOSITIONS/RECORDINGS
View No. 1
Piano, synthesizer, voice Composed for
Ping Chong's <u>AM/AM</u>

View No. 2
Solo voice, synthesizer

**OPERAS/MUSICAL THEATER/
SITE-SPECIFIC WORKS**
Silver Lake with Dolmen Music
An installation exhibited at the Neuberger
Museum, State University of New York
at Purchase, New York

FILMS/VIDEOS
Paris
Color, sound, videotape, 26 minutes.
Conceived and performed by Meredith
Monk and Ping Chong Produced and
directed by Mark Lowry and Kathryn
Escher Made in cooperation with the
Walker Art Center, Minneapolis, and
KTCA-TV, Twin Cities Public Television

1983

MUSICAL COMPOSITIONS/RECORDINGS
Tokyo Cha-Cha
Six voices, two electric organs

Engine Steps
Tape collage

2 Men Walking
Three voices, electric organs

The Games
Sixteen voices, synthesizer, keyboards,
Flemish bagpipes, bagpipes, Chinese
horn, Rauschpfeife

Turtle Dreams
Released on ECM New Series, CD, 78118-
212240-2

**OPERAS/MUSICAL THEATER/
SITE-SPECIFIC WORKS**
Turtle Dreams (Cabaret)
For seven performers **FP** Plexus, New York

The Games
In collaboration with Ping Chong. For six-
teen performers Commissioned by the
Schaubühne am Lehniner Platz, West
Berlin **C** and Scenery by Yoshio Yabara
FP Schaubühne am Lehniner Platz,
West Berlin

FILMS/VIDEOS
Mermaid Adventures
Color, silent, 10 minutes, 16mm. Camera by
David Gearey; projected during <u>Turtle
Dreams (Cabaret)</u>

Turtle Dreams (Waltz)
Color, sound, 1³/4- and ¹/2-in. video,
27 minutes. Directed by Ping Chong;
performed by Meredith Monk and Vocal
Ensemble; coproduced by WGBH-Boston

1984

MUSICAL COMPOSITIONS/RECORDINGS
Panda Chant I
Four voices

Panda Chant II
Eight voices

Graduation Song
Sixteen voices Composed for
Ping Chong's <u>A Race</u>

City Songs
Two voices and two keyboards

1985

MUSICAL COMPOSITIONS/RECORDINGS
Book of Days
Twenty-five voices, synthesizer

Window Song
Solo keyboard Composed for
Ping Chong's <u>Nosferatu</u>

Road Songs
Solo voice and string quartet Composed
for the film <u>True Stories</u>, directed by
David Byrne

1986

MUSICAL COMPOSITIONS/RECORDINGS
Scared Song
Solo voice, synthesizer, piano

I Don't Know
Solo voice, piano

Double Fiesta
Solo voice, two pianos

String
Solo voice

Window in 7's
Solo piano

Ellis Island
Two pianos

*Our Lady of Late: The
Vanguard Tapes*
Released on Wergo Records, SM 1058;
previously unrecorded material, 1973

**OPERAS/MUSICAL THEATER/
SITE-SPECIFIC WORKS**
Acts from Under and Above
In collaboration with Lanny Harrison. For
three performers **FP** La Mama Annex,
New York

1987

MUSICAL COMPOSITIONS/RECORDINGS
Duet Behavior
In collaboration with Bobby McFerrin.
Two voices

The Ringing Place
Nine voices

Do You Be
Ten voices, two pianos, synthesizer, violin,
bagpipes; Released on ECM New Series,
CD, 78118-21336-2

**OPERAS/MUSICAL THEATER/
SITE-SPECIFIC WORKS**
The Ringing Place
For nine performers **FP** Next Wave
Festival, Brooklyn Academy of Music,
Brooklyn, New York

<u>Turtle Dreams (Waltz)</u> Photo: Jack Vartoogian

Meredith Monk and Robert Een in <u>Facing North</u>
Photo: T. Junichi

MUSICAL COMPOSITIONS/RECORDINGS
Fayum Music
In collaboration with Nurit Tilles. Voice, hammered dulcimer, double ocarina

Light Songs
Solo voice

FILMS/VIDEOS
Book of Days
Black-and-white and color, sound, 35mm film transferred to video, 74 minutes Director of photography Jerry Pantzer **C** and art direction Yoshio Yabara First screened at the Montreal Festival of New Film and Video, Montreal

1988

1989

MUSICAL COMPOSITIONS/RECORDINGS
Book of Days (film score)
Ten voices, cello, shawm, synthesizer, hammered dulcimer, bagpipe, hurdy-gurdy

Raven, Parlor Games, Cat Breath, and Graveyard Pavane
Solo voice, two pianos Composed for Ellen Fisher's <u>Dreams Within Dreams: The Life of Edgar Allan Poe</u>

FILMS/VIDEOS
Book of Days
Black-and-white and color, sound (stereo/Dolby), 35mm, 74 minutes Director of photography Jerry Pantzer **C** and art direction Yoshio Yabara First screened at New York Film Festival, New York Reformatted for television: video, 55 minutes; in association with <u>Alive From Off Center</u>, New York

MUSICAL COMPOSITIONS/RECORDINGS
Book of Days
Twelve voices, synthesizer, cello, bagpipe, hurdy-gurdy, piano, hammered dulcimer; Released on ECM New Series, CD, 78118-21399-2

Phantom Waltz
Two pianos

Facing North
In collaboration with Robert Een. Two voices, piano, pitch pipe

OPERAS/MUSICAL THEATER/ SITE-SPECIFIC WORKS
Facing North
For two performers **FP** The House Loft, New York

1990

1991

MUSICAL COMPOSITIONS/RECORDINGS
ATLAS: an opera in three parts
Eighteen voices, two keyboards, clarinet, bass clarinet, sheng, bamboo sax, two violins, viola, two cellos, French horn, percussion, shawm, glass harmonica

OPERAS/MUSICAL THEATER/ SITE-SPECIFIC WORKS
ATLAS: an opera in three parts
For twenty-nine performers Commissioned by The Houston Grand Opera, Houston; Walker Art Center, Minneapolis; The Wexner Center for the Arts, Columbus, Ohio; The American Music Theater Festival, Philadelphia; Hancher Auditorium, Iowa City, Iowa **FP** The Wexner Center for the Arts, Columbus, Ohio

MUSICAL COMPOSITIONS/RECORDINGS
Three Heavens and Hells
Four voices

ATLAS: an opera in three parts
Released on ECM New Series, 1993, CD, 78118-21491-2

Facing North
Released on ECM New Series, CD, 78118-21482-2

Return to Earth
For twenty-four voices Released on <u>Eternal Light</u> (anthology of choral music performed by Musica Sacra), Catalyst, CD, 09026-61822-2

1992

1993

MUSICAL COMPOSITIONS/RECORDINGS
Volcano Songs (Duet), St. Petersburg Waltz, and New York Requiem
Two voices, piano Originally presented as the suite <u>Custom Made</u>

Phantom Waltz and Ellis Island
Released on <u>U.S. Choice</u> (anthology of American music performed by Double Edge), CRI, CD, 637

OPERAS/MUSICAL THEATER/ SITE-SPECIFIC WORKS
Street Corner Pierrot
Solo dance **M** Donald Ashwander **FP** West Kortwright Center, East Meredith, New York Choreography for Donald Ashwander's <u>Particular People</u>

Evanescence
In collaboration with Lanny Harrison. Dance duet **M** Donald Ashwander **FP** West Kortwright Center, East Meredith, New York Choreography for Donald Ashwander's <u>Particular People</u>

MUSICAL COMPOSITIONS/RECORDINGS
American Archeology #1: Roosevelt Island
Seventy voices, organ, bass, medieval drum, shawm

Volcano Songs (Solo)
Solo voice, with taped voices and piano

St. Petersburg Waltz
Solo piano version

OPERAS/MUSICAL THEATER/ SITE-SPECIFIC WORKS
Volcano Songs
Solo Commissioned by Walker Art Center, Minneapolis; The House Foundation for the Arts, New York; PS 122, New York; Hancher Auditorium, Iowa City, Iowa **FP** Walker Art Center, Minneapolis

American Archeology #1
For seventy performers Commissioned by Walker Art Center, Minneapolis; The House Foundation for the Arts, New York; Dancing in the Streets, New York; PS 122, New York; Hancher Auditorium, Iowa City, Iowa **FP** at three sites in New York: Roosevelt Island, Lighthouse Park, and Renwick Ruin

1994

1995

MUSICAL COMPOSITIONS/RECORDINGS
Nightfall
Sixteen voices

Denkai and Krikiki Chants
Four voices

Meredith Monk
Photo: Dona Ann McAdams

MUSICAL COMPOSITIONS/RECORDINGS

The Politics of Quiet: a music theater oratorio
Twelve voices, two keyboards, French horn, violin, bowed psaltry

Monk and the Abbess: The Music of Meredith Monk and Hildegard von Bingen
Released on BMG/Catalyst (performed by Musica Sacra), CD, 09026-68329-2

OPERAS/MUSICAL THEATER/ SITE-SPECIFIC WORKS

The Politics of Quiet: a music theater oratorio
For fourteen performers Commissioned by The House Foundation for the Arts, New York; Lied Center for the Performing Arts, Lincoln, Nebraska; Walker Art Center, Minneapolis; Pittsburgh Dance Council and Three Rivers Arts Festival, Pittsburgh **FP** PS 122, New York

A Celebration Service
For twenty performers A nonsectarian worship service commissioned by The American Guild of Organists **FP** James Memorial Chapel, Union Theological Seminary, New York

MUSICAL COMPOSITIONS/RECORDINGS
Birthday Song #3
Solo voice

170   **1996**   **1998**

1997

MUSICAL COMPOSITIONS/RECORDINGS
Steppe Music
Solo piano

Volcano Songs
Four voices, piano; Released on ECM New Series, CD, 78118-21589-2

Meredith Monk and Vocal Ensemble in
<u>A Celebration Service</u>   Photo: Virginia Dimsev

Abbreviations:

M Music by
T Text by
S Scenery by
C Costumes by
L Lighting by
P Performed by
FP First performance

EARLY WORK

Pas de Deux for Two 1973
In collaboration with Arnie Zane. **M** Benny Goodman **FP** 137 Washington Street, Binghamton, New York

Dances for a Third American Century 1974
In collaboration with Lois Welk. For twenty-five dancers **FP** Albany, Stony Brook, Warwick, New York

A Dance with Durga Devi 1974
M Tibetan Temple Chants and Bessie Smith **FP** American Dance Asylum, Binghamton, New York

Negroes for Sale 1974
Audio collage by Bill T. Jones **S** Arnie Zane **FP** Collective for Living Cinema, New York

Entrances 1974
FP American Dance Asylum, Binghamton, New York

Track Dance 1974
For fifty dancers **S** Don Bosch **M** Lou Grassi **FP** State University of New York, Binghamton

Could Be Dance 1975
FP American Dance Asylum, Binghamton, New York

Dancing and Video in Binghamton 1975
In collaboration with American Dance Asylum, Peer Bode, and Meryl Blackman. **FP** Experimental Television Center, Binghamton, New York

Across the Street There Is a Highway 1975
For twenty-eight dancers, including many Jones family members **FP** The Farm, San Francisco

Women in Drought 1975
FP American Dance Asylum, Binghamton, New York

Across the Street 1975
In collaboration with Arnie Zane. **T** Bill T. Jones, film by Arnie Zane **FP** American Dance Asylum, Binghamton, New York

Impersonations 1975
FP American Dance Asylum, Binghamton, New York

Everybody Works/All Beasts Count 1975
Two versions: Solo **M** Jesse Fuller sang an a capella duet by Arnie Zane and Lynda Berry **FP** Clark Center, New York; Ensemble version for fourteen dancers Masks by Bill T. Jones **FP** American Dance Asylum, Binghamton, New York

For You
FP Daniel Nagrin Dance Theatre, New York

Stomps
FP Daniel Nagrin Dance Theatre, New York

Walk
FP Daniel Nagrin Dance Theatre, New York

A Man
FP Daniel Nagrin Dance Theatre, New York

Asymmetry: Every Which Way
For six performers **M** Lou Grassi **S** Bill T. Jones and Peer Bode **FP** Roberson Art Center, Sears Harkness Theatre, Binghamton, New York

Da Sweet Streak Ta Love Land
For six dancers **M** Otis Redding Mask by Bill T. Jones **FP** Clark Center, New York

1977

1978

Whosedebabedoll? Baby Doll??
In collaboration with Arnie Zane. **T** Bill T. Jones and Arnie Zane **FP** American Dance Asylum, Binghamton, New York

Floating the Tongue
Solo improvisation in four phases **FP** Kent School for Boys, Kent, Connecticut

Naming Things Is Only the Intention to Make Things
Duet with jazz vocalist Jeanne Lee **T,C** Bill T. Jones **FP** The Kitchen, New York

Progresso
S Bill T. Jones **FP** The Kitchen, New York

By the Water
T and movement in collaboration with Sheryl Sutton. **S** Charles Kiesling, in collaboration with Sheryl Sutton and Bill T. Jones **FP** American Dance Asylum, Binghamton, New York

Monkey Run Road
In collaboration with Arnie Zane. **M** Helen Thorington **T** Bill T. Jones **S,C** Bill T. Jones and Arnie Zane **FP** American Dance Asylum, Binghamton, New York

Echo
M Helen Thorington **FP** The Kitchen, New York

Addition
L Carol Mullins **FP** Washington Square Church, New York

Circle in Distance
T and movement in collaboration with Sheryl Sutton **S** Bill T. Jones and Sheryl Sutton **L** Carol Mullins **FP** Washington Square Church, New York

1979

1980

Dance in the Trees
Environmental work for ten community members and two musicians **M** Jeff Cohan and Pete Simonsen **C** Renata Sack and Bill T. Jones **FP** Hartman Land Reserve, Cedar Falls, Iowa

Open Places: A Dance in June
Environmental work for twenty-one adults and children performed in four park settings **M** Dan Hummel, Mark Gaurmond, and Thomas Berry **C** Renata Sack and Bill T. Jones **FP** Waterloo, Iowa

Untitled Duet
With Sherry Satenstrom **M** Dan Hummel, Marcia Miget, and Dartanyan Brown **FP** Recreation Center, Waterloo, Iowa

Balancing the World
Two versions: Duet with Julie West **FP** Iowa Amerika House, Berlin; Ensemble version for six dancers **L** William Yehle **FP** University of Northern Iowa, Cedar Falls

Sweeps
In collaboration with Arnie Zane. Video by Meryl Blackman **S** Rosina Kuhn (painting) **FP** Zürich

Blauvelt Mountain
In collaboration with Arnie Zane. **M** Helen Thorington **S** Bill Katz **L** William Yehle **FP** Dance Theater Workshop, New York

Sisyphus
M Helen Thorington **T,S** Bill T. Jones **FP** Terrace Theater, Kennedy Center, Washington, D.C.

Social Intercourse: Pilgrim's Progress
Assisted by Arnie Zane **M** Joe Hannon **T** and lyrics by Bill T. Jones, additional material composed and sung by Johari Briggs, Rhodessa Jones, and Flo Brown **FP** Stewart Theatre, American Dance Festival, Duke University, Raleigh, North Carolina

Break
M George Lewis **S** Local grade school children **P** Twenty-five dancers **FP** Nicollet Island Ampitheatre, sponsored by Walker Art Center, Minneapolis

Valley Cottage
In collaboration with Arnie Zane **M** Helen Thorington **T** Bill T. Jones and Arnie Zane **S** Bill Katz Slides by Arnie Zane **L** William Yehle **FP** Dance Theater Workshop, New York

Io
Part One: Prologue Performance for Bicycle, Voice, Slide, and Dress **T** Bill T. Jones **L** William Yehle Part Two **S** Bill T. Jones **FP** Dance Theater Workshop, New York

Ah! Break It!
M Jalalu Calvert Nelson with recorded chants by Bill T. Jones **P** Twelve dancers **FP** Werkcetrum Dans, Rotterdam, The Netherlands

1981

1982

Three Dances
M Mozart and Peter Gordon **T** Bill T. Jones **FP** Harvard University, Cambridge, Massachusetts

Rotary Action
Collaboration with Arnie Zane **M** Peter Gordon **L** William Yehle **FP** New Dance, New York, and Vienna Festival, Vienna

Dance for the Convergence of Three Rivers
In collaboration with Arnie Zane. **M** George Lewis **FP** Three Rivers Arts Festival, Pittsburgh, Pennsylvania

Long Distance
Solo, with Keith Haring (who painted during the performance) **FP** The Kitchen, New York

Shared Distance
Duet with Julie West **FP** The Kitchen, New York

Duet x 2
Danced first with Rob Besserer, then with Brian Arsenault **M** Bach air sung by Brian Arsenault **FP** The Kitchen, New York

BTJ

Intuitive Momentum
In collaboration with Arnie Zane. **M** Max
Roach and Connie Crothers **S** Robert
Longo **C** Ronald Kolodzie **L** Craig
Miller **FP** Brooklyn Academy of Music,
Brooklyn, New York

Fever Swamp
M Peter Gordon **S,C** Bill Katz **L** Rick
Nelson Commissioned by the Alvin
Ailey American Dance Theater
FP Santa Monica Civic Auditorium,
Santa Monica, California

Naming Things
In collaboration with Phillip Mallory Jones
and David Hammons. **M** Miles Davis
and traditional funeral dirge; performed
with Rhonda Moore and Poonie
Dodson **FP** Just Above Midtown
Gallery, New York

21
Solo performance (Re-created for video
with Tom Bowes, 1984) **FP** Recreation
Center, Waterloo, Iowa

Corporate Whimsy
M Byron Rulon **P** First Avenue Dance
Group **FP** Tisch School of the Arts,
New York University, New York

Casino
Extended company work with twelve students
M Peter Gordon **S** Robert Longo
FP Ohio University, Athens, Ohio

172 **1983**

1, 2, 3
M Carl Stone **L** Robert Wierzel
S,C Bill T. Jones **FP** The Joyce
Theater, New York

Holzer Duet . . . Truisms
Duet with Lawrence Goldhuber **T** Jenny
Holzer; Audio collage by Bill T. Jones
L Robert Wierzel **FP** The Joyce Theater,
New York

M.A.K.E.
T Bill T. Jones and Arnie Zane **S** Bill T.
Jones **L** Robert Wierzel **FP** The Joyce
Theater, New York

Pastiche
M James Brown, Eric Dolphy **T** Bill T.
Jones, William Shakespeare, and Edith
Sitwell Visuals: found latern slides from
Arnie Zane **L** Robert Wierzel Crown:
Marcel Fieve **FP** The Joyce Theater,
New York

1985

Holzer Duet . . . Truisms

Where the Queen Stands Guard
In collaboration with Arnie Zane.
M "Verdiana" by Vittorio Rieti, per-
formed by the St. Luke's Chamber
Ensemble **S,C** Frank L. Viner **L** Robert
Wierzel Commissioned by the St.
Luke's Chamber Ensemble **FP** Triplex
Theater, Borough of Manhattan
Community of College, New York

Red Room
M Stuart Argabright and Robert Longo
S Robert Longo Commissioned for
Robert Longo's KILLINGANGELS
FP Rockwell Hall, Buffalo, New York

1987

Don't Lose Your Eye
M Sonny Boy Williamson and Paul Lansky
Commissioned for Path Dance
Company **FP** Baltimore, Maryland

Forsythia
Duet with Arthur Aviles **M** Dufay
T Arnie Zane **L** Robert Wierzel
FP The Joyce Theater, New York

La Grand Fête
M Paul Lansky **C** and masks: Dain Marcus
L Robert Wierzel **FP** The Joyce Theater,
New York

It Takes Two
M Ray Charles, Betty Carter **L** Raymond
Dooley Commissioned by Terry Creach
and Stephen Koester **FP** Dance Theater
Workshop, New York

Absence
M Krzystof Penderecki, Hector Berlioz
C Marina Harris **S,L** Robert Wierzel
FP The Joyce Theater, New York

D-Man in the Waters
M Felix Mendelssohn **C** Damien
Acquavella and the Company **L** Robert
Wierzel Commissioned in part by St.
Luke's Chamber Orchestra **FP** The Joyce
Theater, New York

Untitled
A dance for video, filmed and edited by
Sanborn, Perillo for Alive From Off
Center at Alive TV, St. Paul, Minnesota

1989

1984

Dances with Brahms
Two versions: **P** Bill T. Jones and three
dancers **M** Johannes Brahms **FP** Paula
Cooper Gallery, New York; Solo
C Jimmy Myers **FP** Leuven, Belgium

Freedom of Information
In collaboration with Arnie Zane. **M** David
Cunningham **T** Bill T. Jones **S** and
video by Gretchen Bender **L** William
DeMull **FP** Theatre de la Ville, Paris

Secret Pastures
In collaboration with Arnie Zane. **M** Peter
Gordon **S** Keith Haring **C** Willi Smith
Hair, makeup, and painting of
Fabricated Man by Marcel Fieve **L** Stan
Pressner **FP** Brooklyn Academy of
Music, Brooklyn, New York

1986

Virgil Thompson Études
M Virgil Thompson **C** Louise Nevelson
and William Katz **L** Craig Miller
Commissioned for Virgil Thompson's
ninetieth birthday celebration
FP Chanterelle, New York

Animal Trilogy
In collaboration with Arnie Zane.
M Conlon Nancarrow **S** Cletus
Johnson **C** Bill Katz **L** Robert Wierzel
Commissioned in part by the Brooklyn
Academy of Music, Brooklyn, New York
FP Biennale Internationale de la Danse,
Lyon, France

1988

The History of Collage
In collaboration with Arnie Zane
M Charles R. Amirkhanian and "Blue"
Gene Tyranny **L** Robert Wierzel
FP The Ohio Theater, Cleveland

Chatter
M Paul Lansky **L** Robert Wierzel
FP American Dance Festival, Durham,
North Carolina

Soon
M Kurt Weill, Bessie Smith **L** Robert
Wierzel **FP** Celebrate Brooklyn Festival,
Prospect Park, Brooklyn, New York

1990

**Last Supper at Uncle Tom's
Cabin/The Promised Land**
M Julius Hemphill **T** R. Justice Allen,
Ann T. Greene, Bill T. Jones, Estella
Jones, Heidi Latsky, and Sojourner
Truth **S,C** Huck Snyder **L** Robert
Wierzel Co-commissioned by Walker
Art Center, Minneapolis **FP** Next Wave
Festival, Brooklyn Academy of Music,
Brooklyn, New York Co-commissioned
by Walker Art Center, Minneapolis

Another History of Collage
M Charles R. Amirkhanian and "Blue"
Gene Tyranny **L** Robert Wierzel
FP Diversions Dance Company,
Cardiff, Wales

THEATER WORKS
New Year
Choreographed for productions at Houston
Grand Opera and Glyndebourne
Festival Opera, under the direction
of Sir Peter Hall

Mother of Three Sons
Directed and choreographed for produc-
tions at Munich Biennale, New York
City Opera, and Houston Grand Opera

Perfect Courage
Codirected with Rhodessa Jones **P** Bill T.
Jones, Rhodessa Jones, Idris Ackamoor
Co-commissioned by the Walker Art
Center, Minneapolis, and Festival 2000,
San Francisco

Video still from Animal Trilogy

Havoc
M John Bergamo **C** Liz Prince **L** Robert Wierzel **FP** Joyce Theater, New York

Havoc in Heaven
M John Bergamo **C** Liz Prince **L** Robert Wierzel **FP** Berkshire Ballet, Albany, New York

1991

After Black Room
By Arnie Zane; restaged by Bill T. Jones
S Robert Wierzel after Arnie Zane
L Robert Wierzel **FP** Cannes Festivale Internationale de la Danse, Cannes, France

Last Night on Earth
M Kurt Weill, Nina Simone, and Koko Taylor **C** Rifat Ozbeck **L** Robert Wierzel **FP** The Joyce Theater, New York

Achilles Loved Patroclus
M John Oswald Audiotaped narrative: Derek Jacobi reading The Iliad **C** Liz Prince **S,L** Robert Wierzel **FP** The Joyce Theater, New York

War Between the States
M Charles Ives **C** Isaac Mizrahi **L** Robert Wierzel **FP** The Joyce Theater, New York

There Were So Many . . .
M John Cage **C** Linda Pratt and Jean-Claude Mastroianni **L** Robert Wierzel **FP** The Joyce Theater, New York

And the Maiden
M Bessie Jones and Group from "Georgia Sea Island Songs" **C** Liz Prince **S** Bill T. Jones **L** Robert Wierzel **FP** The Joyce Theater, New York

Just You
M Frank Loesser, Harry Woods, Coslow Johnston, Klages-Greer, Cole Porter, and Hoffman-Manning **L** Robert Wierzel **FP** The Joyce Theater, New York

1993

War Between the States
Photo: Michael O'Neill

New Duet
M John Oswald, Laurel McDonald **C** Olga Maslova **L** Gregory Bain **FP** RomaEuropa Festival, Rome

Degga
In collaboration with Toni Morrison and Max Roach. **L** Robert Wierzel **S** Nari Ward **C** Ilona Somogy **P** Alice Tully Hall, Lincoln Center, New York

24 Frames per Second
M John Oswald **FP** Lyon Opera Ballet, Lyon, France

1995

Duet
M traditional music from Madagascar, Iran, and Ivory Coast **C** Olga Maslova **L** Gregory Bain **FP** RomaEuropa Festival, Rome

Some Songs
M Jacques Brel **C** Fernando Sanchez and Olga Maslova **S** Bill T. Jones **L** Gregory Bain **FP** Le Havre, France

Green and Blue
M Mozart **S** Bjorn G. Amelan **C** Janet Wong and Bill T. Jones **L** Robert Wierzel Commissioned by Lyon Opera Ballet **FP** Lyon Opera House, Lyon, France

Lisbon
In collaboration with Maya Saffrin.
M Laurel McDonald, with sound collage by Gregory Bain **C** the Company **L** Robert Wierzel **FP** Emerson Majestic Theater, Boston

We Set Out Early . . . Visibility Was Poor
M Igor Stravinsky, John Cage, Peteris Vasks **C** Liz Prince **S** Bjorn G. Amelan **L** Robert Wierzel **FP** The John F. Kennedy Center for Performing Arts, Eisenhower Theater, Washington, D.C.

Sonata and . . .
M Rodion Schedrin Commissioned by José Navas **FP** Vienna Dance Festival, Vienna

1997

1992

Broken Wedding
M Klezmer Conservatory Band **C,S** Liz Prince **L** Robert Wierzel Commissioned by the Boston Ballet **FP** The Wang Center, Boston

Die Offnung
M John Oswald **C** Liz Prince **L** Robert Wierzel Commissioned by the Berlin Opera Ballet **FP** Deutsche Opera Berlin, Berlin

Love Defined
M Daniel Johnston **S** Donald Baechler **C** Bill Katz **L** Robert Wierzel Commissioned by the Lyon Opera Ballet **FP** Maison de la Danse, Lyon, France

Our Respected Dead
M Daniel Johnston **S** Donald Baechler **C** Bill Katz **L** Robert Wierzel **FP** The Joyce Theater, New York

Fête
M Paul Lansky **C** Liz Prince **L** Robert Wierzel **FP** The Joyce Theater, New York

THEATER WORKS
Lost in the Stars
Director for the Boston Lyric Opera, Boston

1994

Still/Here
Media environment: Gretchen Bender
M "Still": Kenneth Frazelle, traditional sung by Odetta, the Lark String Quartet, and Bill Finizio; "Here": Vernon Reid **T** Participants of survival workshops and Lawrence Goldhuber **C** Liz Prince **L** Robert Wierzel Co-commissioned by Walker Art Center, Minneapolis **FP** Biennale Internationale de la Danse, Lyon, France

I Want to Cross Over
M traditional gospel music sung by Liz McComb **S** Donald Baechler **C** Bill Katz **L** Robert Wierzel Commissioned by Lyon Opera Ballet **FP** Lyon Opera Ballet, Lyon Opera House

THEATER WORKS
Dream on Monkey Mountain
Directed for the Guthrie Theater, Minneapolis

1996

Ursonate
In collaboration with Darla Villani. Sound poem by Kurt Schwitters **C** Byron Lars **L** Robert Wierzel **FP** The Joyce Theater, New York

Bill and Laurie: About Five Rounds
In collaboration with Laurie Anderson. Video by Chris Kondek **L** Robert Wierzel **FP** The Joyce Theater, New York

Ballad
Poems written and read by Dylan Thomas **C** Liz Prince **L** Robert Wierzel **FP** The Joyce Theater, New York

Blue Phrase
M Eric Dolphy **C** Olga Maslova **L** Robert Wierzel **FP** The Joyce Theater, New York

Love Re-Defined
M Daniel Johnston **S** Donald Baechler **C** Liz Prince **L** Robert Wierzel **FP** The Joyce Theater, New York

Sur la Place
M Jacques Brel **C** Fernando Sanchez **S** Bill T. Jones **L** Robert Wierzel **FP** Cour d'Honneur, Festival D'Avignon, Avignon, France

---

1998

Étude
Solo **M** Beethoven **L** Gregory Bain **FP** Classical Action Benefit, BAM Majestic Theater, Brooklyn, New York

Nowhere but Here
M Igor Stravinsky and Peteris Vasks **S** Bjorn G. Amelan **L** Robert Wierzel **FP** Diversions Dance Company, Cardiff, Wales

Selected Reading List

Merce Cunningham

Adam, Judy. Dancers on a Plane: Cage Cunningham Johns. New York: Alfred A. Knopf; London: Thames & Hudson; in association with Anthony d'Offay Gallery, 1990.

Cunningham, Merce. Changes: Notes on Choreography. Edited by Frances Starr. New York: Something Else Press, 1968.

Cunningham, Merce, in conversation with Jacqueline Lesschaeve. The Dancer and the Dance, rev. ed. New York and London: Marion Boyers, 1991.

Klosty, James, ed. Merce Cunningham. New York: E.P. Dutton & Co., Inc., 1975.

Vaughan, David, ed. "Merce Cunningham: Creative Elements." Choreography and Dance: An International Journal, vol. 4 (1997).

Vaughan, David, and Melissa Harris, ed. Merce Cunningham. Fifty Years. New York: Aperture Foundation, Inc., 1997.

Meredith Monk

Baker, Robb. "New Worlds for Old: The Visionary Art of Meredith Monk." American Theater Magazine (October 1984): p. 4.

Berger, Mark, and Westwater, Angela. "Meredith Monk: A Metamorphic Theatre." Artforum (May 1973): pp. 57–63.

Jowitt, Deborah, ed. Meredith Monk. Baltimore and London: The Johns Hopkins University Press, 1997.

Monk, Meredith, Geoff Smith, Nicola Smith. New Voices: American Composers Talk About Their Music. Portland, Oregon: Amadeus Press, 1995: pp. 183–194.

Shapiro, Laura. "Games That Meredith Plays." Newsweek (October 29, 1984): pp. 124–125.

Spector, Nancy. "The Anti-Narrative: Meredith Monk's Theater." Parkett (Zürich), no. 23 (1990): pp. 110–113.

Bill T. Jones

Gates, Henry Louis, Jr. "The Body Politic." The New Yorker, vol. LXX, no. 39 (November 28, 1994): pp. 112–124.

Jones, Bill T., with Peggy Gillespie. Last Night on Earth. New York: Pantheon Books, 1995.

Killacky, John. "The Moving Visions of Bill T. Jones." Inside Arts, Association of Performing Arts Presenters, vol. 2, no. 3 (September 1990): pp. 34–38.

Laine, Barry. "Trendy Twosome." Ballet News. vol. 7, no. 2 (August 1985): pp. 22–25.

Washington, Eric K. "Sculpture in Flight, a conversation with Bill T. Jones." Transition 62 (1993): pp. 190–191.

Zimmer, Elizabeth. "Bill T. Jones and Arnie Zane: Solid Citizens of Post-Modernism." Dancemagazine, vol. LVIII, no. 10 (October 1984): pp. 56–60.

Zimmer, Elizabeth, and Susan Quasha, eds. Body Against Body. The Dance and Other Collaborations of Bill T. Jones and Arnie Zane. Barrytown, New York: Station Hill Press, 1989.

Walker Art Center Board of Directors, 1997–1998

Published in conjunction with the exhibition
<u>Art Performs Life: Merce Cunningham/Meredith Monk/Bill T. Jones</u>
presented by the Walker Art Center, June 28–September 20, 1998

<u>Art Performs Life: Merce Cunningham/Meredith Monk/Bill T. Jones</u> is made possible by
generous support from AT&T.

Additional support for this exhibition is provided by the National Endowment for the Arts, Dayton's Frango® Fund,
Goldman, Sachs & Co., and Voyageur Companies. Related performances and residency activities are
supported by the National Endowment for the Arts, Sage and John Cowles, Arts Midwest Performing
Arts Touring Fund, Heartland Arts Fund, Martha and Bruce Atwater, the Rehael Fund–Roger L. Hale/
Eleanor L. Hall of The Minneapolis Foundation, Harriet and Ed Spencer, Penny and Mike Winton,
Gertrude Lippincott Fund, Martha Ann Davies, Constance Mayeron and Charles Fuller Cowles, Mr. and
Mrs. Jay Cowles, Joanne and Philip Von Blon, Margaret and Angus Wurtele, Susan and Paul DeNuccio,
Suzanne and Ted Zorn, Katherine and Robert Goodale, Judith and Jerome Ingber, Suzanne Weil,
Priscilla Goldstein, and Deanie and Frank Pass.
This exhibition is part of the Walker Art Center's "New Definitions/New Audiences" initiative. This museum-wide project
to engage visitors in a reexamination of 20th-century art is made possible by the Lila Wallace-Reader's
Digest Fund.
This book was made possible in part by a grant from the Andrew W. Mellon Foundation in support of Walker Art
Center publications.
Major support for Walker Art Center programs is provided by the Minnesota State Arts Board through an appropriation
by the Minnesota State Legislature, the Lila Wallace-Reader's Digest Fund, The Bush Foundation, the
National Endowment for the Arts, Target Stores, Dayton's, and Mervyn's by the Dayton Hudson
Foundation, The McKnight Foundation, the General Mills Foundation, Coldwell Banker Burnet, the
Institute of Museum and Library Services, the American Express Minnesota Philanthropic Program, the
Honeywell Foundation, The Cargill Foundation, The Regis Foundation, The St. Paul Companies, Inc.,
U.S. Bank, the 3M Foundation, and the members of the Walker Art Center.
Northwest Airlines, Inc. is the official airline of the Walker Art Center.

Lenders to the Exhibition

The Cunningham Dance Foundation
Bill T. Jones/Arnie Zane Dance Company and the Foundation for Dance Promotion
Meredith Monk/The House Foundation for the Arts, Inc.

Gretchen Bender
Molly Davies
Peter Gordon
Estate of Keith Haring, New York
Estate of Julius Hemphill/Subito Music Corp.
Cletus Johnson
Robert and Jane Meyerhoff
Bruce Nauman
The New York Public Library, Music Division
Scott Padden, Aperture, New York
Margarete Roeder Gallery, New York
Barbara Schwartz, New York
UCR/California Museum of Photography, University of California, Riverside
Johanna VanDerBeek
The Andy Warhol Museum
Larry Warsh, Art Knowledge Corporation, New York

Reproduction Credits

Images for Merce Cunningham courtesy Merce Cunningham/Merce Cunningham Dance Company: 22–42, 44–45, 46 (bottom), 47–55, 57, 60–61, 158–163, 165; Images for Bill T. Jones courtesy Bill T. Jones/Arnie Zane Dance Company/Foundation for Dance Promotion: 118–124, 126–134, 136, 138–148, 150–151, 156–157, 170, 172–173; Images for Meredith Monk courtesy Meredith Monk/The House Foundation for the Arts, Inc.: cover, inside back cover, 68–78, 80–97, 100 (bottom left), 100–101 (bottom center), 104–115, 166–167, 169–170.

In addition, the publisher wishes to acknowledge the following for images reproduced in this book: Michael Blackwood Productions, Inc.: 172 (top); Tom Brazil: 149; Glenn Halvorson, Walker Art Center: inside front cover, 54 (bottom left), 145; Estate of Keith Haring, New York: 125; Comme des Garçons: 62–63; Credo Interactive: 64–65; Robert and Jane Meyerhoff: 56; The Estate of Peter Moore/VAGA, New York: 79, 100–103, 105 (top), 107 (bottom left); UCR/California Museum of Photography, University of California, Riverside: 137; Barbara Schwartz, New York: 46 (inset), 47 (inset); David Smith: 152–153; © Jack Vartoogian: 46 (top), 58–59, 106, 154–155, 164, 168; Walker Art Center Archives: 8–9, 11, 13, 15, 110 (top), 111 (top right); and Robert Withers: 98–99.

Curators Philippe Vergne, Siri Engberg, and Kellie Jones
Curatorial Intern Jenelle Porter
Designer Conny Purtill
Editors Pamela Johnson and Kathleen McLean
Publications Manager Michelle Piranio
Typeface Minion, CITIZEN
Paper Finch Fine Bright White VHF 80 lb. text and Classic Crest Solar White 130 lb. cover

Art Performs Life: Merce Cunningham/Meredith Monk/Bill T. Jones

Printed in the United States of America by Print Craft, Inc., Minneapolis

Available through D.A.P./Distributed Art Publishers

155 Avenue of the Americas, 2nd floor, New York, New York 10013

First Edition © 1998 Walker Art Center

Library of Congress Cataloging-in-Publication Data

Art performs life : Merce Cunningham, Meredith Monk, Bill T. Jones —
    1st ed.
        p. cm.
        Published in conjunction with exhibition to be held at Walker Art Center, June 28–Sept. 20, 1998.
    Includes interviews with Cunningham, Monk, and Jones.
        Includes bibliographical references (p.).
        ISBN 0-935640-56-8
        1. Cunningham, Merce—Interviews. 2. Monk, Meredith—Interviews. 3. Jones, Bill T.—Interviews. 4. Dancers—United States—Interviews. 5. Choreographers—United States—Interviews. 6. Dance costume—Catalogs. 7. Theaters—Stage-setting and scenery—catalogs. 8. Dance—Film catalogs. 9. Music scores—Catalogs.
I. Cunningham, Merce. II. Monk, Meredith. III. Jones, Bill T. IV. Walker Art Center
GV1785.A1A78   1998
792.8'092'273—dc21
                                          98-7401
                                          CIP